Letts and Lonsdale

GCSE Success

Workbook

Edexcel Mathematics Foundation

Fiona C. Mapp

Contents

Number

Algebra

Shape, Space and Measures

Handling Data

If you are following the modular specification (2381), the numbers in brackets indicate which unit(s) the content of each page is relevant to.

Homework diary

TOPIC	SCORE
Number revision	/25
Numbers	/41
Positive and negative numbers	/27
Working with numbers	/41
Fractions	/40
Decimals	/32
Percentages 1	/30
Percentages 2	/33
Fractions, decimals and percentages	/29
Approximations and using a calculator	/35
Ratio	/28
Indices	/48
Algebra 1	/27
Algebra 2	/45
Equations 1	/55
Equations 2 and inequalities	/29
Number patterns and sequences	/34
Straight line graphs	/24
Curved graphs	/21
Interpreting graphs	/17
Shapes	/26
Solids	/20
Symmetry and constructions	/22
Angles	/27
Bearings and scale drawings	/22
Transformations 1	/22
Transformations 2	/18
Loci and coordinates	/21
Pythagoras' theorem	/28
Measures and measurement 1	/22
Measures and measurement 2	/36
Area of 2D shapes	/29
Volume of 3D shapes	/32
Collecting data	/18
Representing data	/23
Scatter diagrams and correlation	/21
Averages 1	/29
Averages 2	/22
Probability 1	/28
Probability 2	/23

Exam Hints

Planning and revising

- Mathematics should be revised **actively**. You should be doing **more than just reading**.
- Find out the dates of your first mathematics examination. Make an examination and revision timetable.
- After completing a topic in school, go through the topic again in the **GCSE Success Guide**. Copy out the **main points**, **results** and **formulae** into a notebook or use a **highlighter** to emphasise them.
- Try and write out the **key points** from **memory**. Check what you have written and see if there are any differences.
- Revise in short bursts of about **30 minutes**, followed by a **short break**.
- Learn **facts** from your exercise books, notebooks and the **Success Guide**. **Memorise** any formula you need to learn.
- Learn with a friend to make it easier and more fun!
- Do the **multiple choice** and **quiz-style** questions in this book and check your solutions to see how much you know.
- Once you feel **confident** that you know the topic, do the **GCSE**-style questions in this book. **Highlight** the key words in the question, **plan** your answer and then go back and **check** that you have answered the question.
- **Make a note** of any topics that you do not understand and **go back through the notes** again.

Different types of questions

- On the **GCSE Mathematics papers** you will have several types of questions:

  Calculate – In these questions you need to work out the answer. Remember that it is important to show full working out.

  Explain – These questions want you to explain, with a mathematical reason or calculation, what the answer is.

  Show – These questions usually require you to show, with mathematical justification, what the answer is.

  Write down or state – These questions require no explanation or working out.

  Prove – These questions want you to set out a concise logical argument, making the reasons clear.

  Deduce – These questions make use of an earlier answer to establish a result.

On the day

- **Follow the instructions** on the exam paper. Make sure that you understand what any **symbols** mean.
- Make sure that you **read the question** carefully so that you give the answer that an examiner wants.
- Always **show your working**; you may pick up some marks even if the final answer is wrong.
- Do **rough calculations** to check your answers and make sure that they are **reasonable**.
- When carrying out a calculation, **do not round the answer until the end**, otherwise your final answer will not be as accurate as is needed.
- Lay out your working **carefully** and **concisely**. Write down the calculations that you are going to make. You usually get marks for showing a **correct method**.
- Make your drawings and graphs **neat** and **accurate**.
- Know what is on the **formula sheet** and make sure that you **learn** those formulae that are not on it.
- If you cannot do a question **leave it out** and **go back** to it at the end.
- Keep an eye on the time. Allow enough time to check through your answers.
- If you finish early, check through everything very carefully and try and fill in the gaps.
- Try and write something even if you are not sure about it. Leaving an empty space will score you no marks.

  In this book, questions which may be answered with a calculator are marked with (C). All the other questions are intended to be answered without the use of a calculator.

Good luck!

Number revision

A

Choose just one answer, a, b, c or d.

1 **Which of these is the largest number?**
1469, 3271, 1059, 3276 (1 mark)

a) 1469 b) 3271
c) 1059 d) 3276

2 **What does the digit 7 in the number 34 718 stand for?** (1 mark)

a) 7 units b) 7 tens
c) 7 hundreds d) 7 thousands

3 **Which number represents fifty-two thousand, four hundred and six?** (1 mark)

a) 52 406 b) 54 206
c) 52 460 d) 5246

4 **What is the third multiple of 7?** (1 mark)

a) 7 b) 14
c) 21 d) 28

5 **Here are some cards.**

3	7	6	4

What is the smallest number you can make with these cards? (1 mark)

a) 7643 b) 3764
c) 3674 d) 3467

Score / 5

B

Answer all parts of the questions.

1 **Write these numbers in words.**

a) 602 .... (1 mark)

b) 5729 .... (1 mark)

2 **Write these numbers in figures.**

a) four hundred and thirty-six .... (1 mark)

b) six million, four hundred and five .... (1 mark)

3 **What value does the digit 3 represent in each of these numbers?**

a) 739 .... (1 mark)

b) 83 147 .... (1 mark)

c) 346 295 .... (1 mark)

4 **Arrange these numbers in order of size, smallest first.**

a) 47, 6, 93, 827, 1436, 75, 102 (2 marks)

....

b) 159, 3692, 4207, 4138, 729, 4879 (2 marks)

....

Score / 11

C

These are GCSE-style questions. Answer all parts of the questions. Show your workings (on separate paper if necessary) and include the correct units in your answers.

1 Here is a list of numbers.

17 170 1700 17 000 170 000 1 700 000

Write down the number from the list which is:

a) seventeen hundred .... (1 mark)

b) one hundred and seventy thousand .... (1 mark)

2 **a) Write the number sixteen thousand, four hundred and thirty-one in figures.** (1 mark)

....

b) Write down the value of the 3 in the number 532 146. (1 mark)

....

c) Write down the smallest even number that can be made from these cards. (1 mark)

[3] [5] [2] [8] ....

3 Here is a number grid.

1	2	3	4
5	6	7	8
9	10	11	12
13	14	15	16
17	18	19	20

a) How many of these numbers are odd? (1 mark)

....

b) Write down the numbers from the grid that are multiples of three. (1 mark)

....

4 **Write these numbers in order of size, smallest first.**

a) 61, 104, 18, 130, 72 (1 mark)

....

b) 19, 62, 407, 397, 18 (1 mark)

....

Score / 9

How well did you do? ✗ 1–8 Try again 9–15 Getting there 16–21 Good work 22–25 Excellent! ✓

For more information on this topic see pages 4–5 of your Success Guide.

Numbers

A Choose just one answer, a, b, c or d.

1 What is the positive square root of 81? (1 mark)

a) 7
b) −9
c) 7
d) 9

2 What is the reciprocal of $\frac{7}{4}$? (1 mark)

a) $\frac{7}{4}$
b) $\frac{4}{7}$
c) 7
d) 4

3 What is the value of 4^2? (1 mark)

a) 12
b) 16
c) 4
d) 64

4 Work out the value of $\sqrt[3]{27}$. (1 mark)

a) 9
b) 6
c) 3
d) 81

5 Calculate the highest common factor of 18 and 24. (1 mark)

a) 6
b) 18
c) 12
d) 432

Score / 5

B Answer all parts of the questions.

1 Say whether each statement is true or false. (4 marks)

a) 2 is the only even prime number. ....
b) 12 is a factor of 6. ....
c) 9 is a factor of 3. ....
d) 1, 2, 4, 6, 12, 24 are the only factors of 24. ....

2 Work out the answers to these questions. (6 marks)

a) $\sqrt{4}$ = ...
b) $\sqrt{100}$ = ...
c) 4^3 = ...
d) $\sqrt[3]{8}$ = ...
e) $\sqrt[3]{-125}$ = ...
f) 15^2 = ...

3 Write 72 as a product of its prime factors. .... (2 marks)

4 The number 180 is written as its prime factors. What are the values of *a* and *b*? (2 marks)

$180 = 2^a \times 3^b \times 5$ .... (2 marks)

5 What is the LCM of 20 and 30? .... (1 mark)

6 What is the HCF of 24 and 40? .... (1 mark)

7 Decide whether this statement is true or false. (1 mark)

$\frac{4}{7}$ is the reciprocal of $1\frac{3}{4}$. ....

Score / 19

NUMBERS
Number

C

These are GCSE-style questions. Answer all parts of the questions. Show your workings (on separate paper if necessary) and include the correct units in your answers.

1 Some numbers are in the cloud below. Choose numbers from the cloud to answer the questions below.

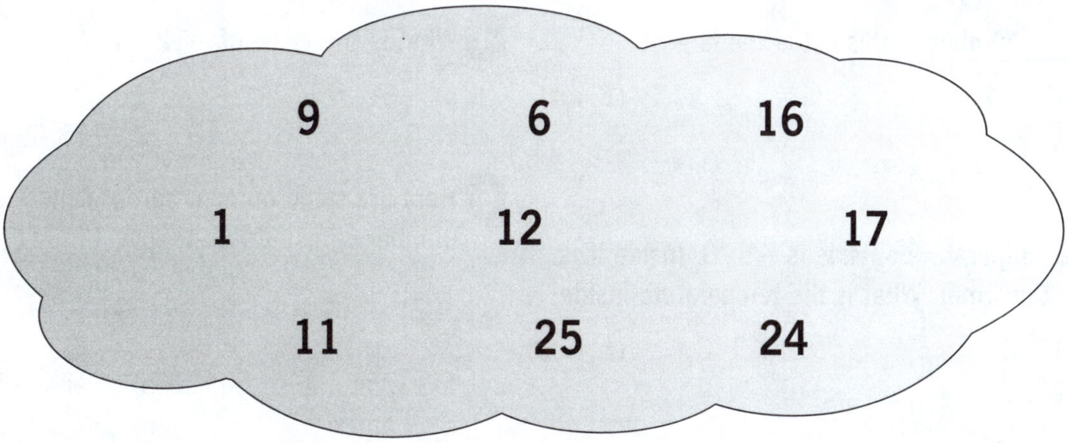

a) Write down the square numbers. .... (1 mark)

b) Write down the numbers which are factors of 24. .... (2 marks)

c) Write down the prime numbers bigger than 7. .... (1 mark)

d) Write down the number that is the reciprocal of $\frac{1}{9}$. .... (1 mark)

2 Explain why $\sqrt{60}$ is less than 8. .... (1 mark)

3 **a)** Express the following numbers as products of their prime factors. (4 marks)

i) 56 ....

ii) 60 ....

b) Find the highest common factor of 56 and 60. .... (2 marks)

c) Find the least common multiple of 56 and 60. .... (2 marks)

4 The number 360 can be written as $2^a \times 3^b \times 5^c$.

Calculate the values of a, b and c. (3 marks)

....

....

Score / 17

How well did you do? 1–11 Try again 12–22 Getting there 23–31 Good work 32–41 Excellent!

For more information on this topic see pages 4–5 of your Success Guide.

Positive and negative numbers

A Choose just one answer, a, b, c or d.

1 **Which number in this list is the largest?**

7, 11, −20, −41 (1 mark)

a) 7 b) 11
c) −20 d) −41

2 **The temperature outside is −5 °C. Inside it is 28 °C warmer. What is the temperature inside?** (1 mark)

a) 17 °C b) 21 °C
c) 23 °C d) 25 °C

3 **If the values on the two number cards are multiplied together, what is the answer?** [−3] [5] (1 mark)

a) −15 b) 2
c) 15 d) 8

4 **What is the value of −12 + (−6)?** (1 mark)

a) −6 b) −20
c) 6 d) −18

5 **Here are some number cards. Which two number cards add up to give 1?** (1 mark)

[−7] [4] [9] [−3]

a) −7 and 4 b) 4 and −3
c) 9 and 4 d) −7 and −3

Score / 5

B Answer all parts of the questions.

1 **Here are some number cards.** [−7] [0] [5] [−3] (3 marks)

a) Choose two of the number cards that add up to give −2. ....
b) Choose two of the number cards that subtract to give −4. ....
c) Choose two of the number cards that multiply to give −35. ....

2 **Draw a line to join each calculation to the correct answer.** (5 marks)

−3 × 4	10
12 ÷ (−2)	−1
−4 − (−3)	−12
−5 × (−2)	4
−20 ÷ (−5)	−6

3 **Work out the answers to the following questions.** (3 marks)

a) (−40) ÷ (−4) = ... b) −7 + (−3) = ... c) 8 − (−6) = ...

4 **Here are some numbers in a number pyramid.** (3 marks)
The number in each rectangle is found by adding the two numbers below.
Complete the number pyramid.

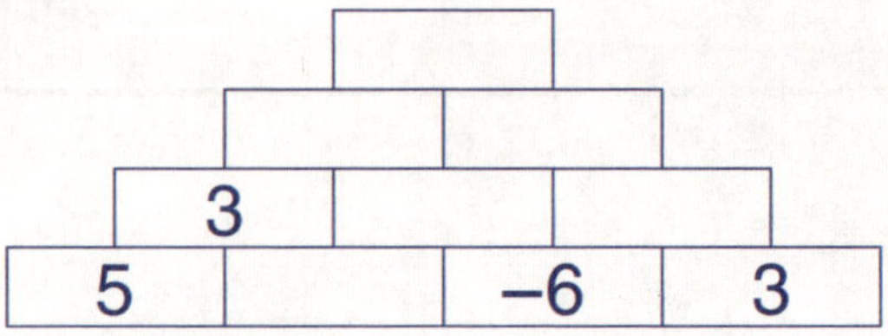

Score / 14

C

These are GCSE-style questions. Answer all parts of the questions. Show your workings (on separate paper if necessary) and include the correct units in your answers.

1 The temperatures at midnight in various cities on one night in December are shown in the table below.

City	Temperature (°C)
Cairo	4
London	−2
New York	−7
Oslo	−14

a) How many degrees warmer is Cairo than Oslo? .... ° (1 mark)

b) i) On the same day the temperature in Sydney is 24 °C warmer than in New York. What is the temperature in Sydney? (2 marks)

.... °

ii) How many degrees colder is it in London than in Sydney? (2 marks)

.... °

2 One evening last winter, the temperature in Swansea was 4 °C, in Manchester it was −2 °C and in Glasgow it was −8 °C.

a) Work out the difference in temperature between Swansea and Glasgow. (1 mark)

.... °

b) The temperature in Manchester increased by 6 °C. Work out the new temperature in Manchester. (1 mark)

.... °

c) The temperature in Glasgow fell by 3 °C. Work out the new temperature in Glasgow. (1 mark)

.... °

Score / 8

How well did you do? ✗ 1–6 Try again 7–14 Getting there 15–21 Good work 22–27 Excellent! ✓

For more information on this topic see pages 6–7 of your Success Guide.

Working with numbers

A

Choose just one answer, a, b, c or d.

1 **Work out the answer to 27 × 100** (1 mark)

a) 27 b) 2700 c) 270 d) 27 000

2 **Work out the answer to 81 ÷ 1000** (1 mark)

a) 81 b) 0.81 c) 0.081 d) 8.1

3 **Work out the answer to 274 + 639** (1 mark)

a) 913 b) 931 c) 879 d) 874

4 **Work out the answer to 1479 − 387** (1 mark)

a) 1192 b) 1092 c) 1112 d) 1012

5 **Work out the answer to 379 × 6** (1 mark)

a) 2072 b) 2174 c) 3274 d) 2274

Score / 5

B

Answer all parts of the questions.

1 **Draw a line from each calculation to the correct answer.** (5 marks)

6 × 10	2400
70 × 1000	70 000
240 ÷ 100	60
600 ÷ 1000	2.4
80 × 30	0.6

2 **Work out the following calculations, showing all your working.** (4 marks)

a) 379 + 42 = ... b) 639 − 274 = ...

c) 5296 × 3 = ... d) 2496 ÷ 3 = ...

3 **Work out the following calculations, showing all your working.** (4 marks)

a) 279 × 26 b) 159 × 48

....

c) 323 ÷ 19 d) 1296 ÷ 27

....

4 **A shop buys 142 sweaters. If each sweater is sold for £62, how much money does the shop take in total?** (2 marks)

....

....

Score / 15

Ⓒ *Indicates that a calculator may be used*

C

These are GCSE-style questions. Answer all parts of the questions. Show your workings (on separate paper if necessary) and include the correct units in your answers.

1 a) Here is Jackie's shopping bill. Complete the totals. (3 marks)

Item	Cost	Number bought	Total cost
Bread	79p	4	....
Milk	72p	2	....
Cleaning fluid	£2.76	2	....

b) Jackie pays using a £5 voucher and the remainder in cash. How much cash does she pay? (1 mark)

....

2 Mrs Sharpe is printing an examination for all Year 10 students.
Each examination uses 16 sheets of paper.

a) There are 186 students in Year 10. How many sheets of paper does she need? (3 marks)

....

....

b) A ream contains 500 sheets of paper.
How many reams of paper does she need to print all the examinations? (2 marks)

....

....

3 The table shows the cost of each of three types of paper.

Plain paper	£2.15
Squared paper	£1.95
Lined paper	£2.70

Simon buys one pack of plain paper and one pack of lined paper. He pays with a £10 note.

a) How much change should he get? (C) (4 marks)

....

....

b) Shezad wants to buy some packs of squared paper. He has £25 to spend.
What is the greatest number of packs of squared paper he can buy? (C) (2 marks)

....

....

4 a) Work out 279 × 48 (3 marks)

....

....

b) Work out 1316 ÷ 28 (3 marks)

....

....

Score / 21

How well did you do? ✗ 1–13 Try again 14–23 Getting there 24–35 Good work 36–41 Excellent! ✓

For more information on this topic see pages 8–9 of your Success Guide.

Fractions

A Choose just one answer, a, b, c or d.

1 Which one of these fractions is equivalent to $\frac{5}{9}$? (1 mark)

a) $\frac{16}{27}$ b) $\frac{9}{18}$
c) $\frac{25}{45}$ d) $\frac{21}{36}$

2 In a class of 24 students, $\frac{3}{8}$ wear glasses. How many students wear glasses? (1 mark)

a) 9
b) 6
c) 3
d) 12

3 Work out the answer to $\frac{5}{9} - \frac{1}{3}$ (1 mark)

a) $\frac{1}{3}$ b) $\frac{2}{9}$
c) $\frac{4}{6}$ d) $\frac{4}{12}$

4 Work out the answer to $\frac{2}{11} \times \frac{7}{9}$ (1 mark)

a) $\frac{14}{11}$ b) $\frac{14}{9}$
c) $\frac{14}{99}$ d) $\frac{2}{99}$

5 Work out the answer to $\frac{3}{10} \div \frac{2}{5}$ (1 mark)

a) $\frac{3}{4}$ b) $\frac{6}{50}$
c) $\frac{6}{15}$ d) $\frac{4}{3}$

Score / 5

B Answer all parts of the questions.

1 Fill in the blanks in these equivalent fractions. (4 marks)

a) $\frac{2}{11} = \frac{4}{\square}$ b) $\frac{4}{7} = \frac{\square}{49}$ c) $\frac{25}{100} = \frac{1}{\square}$ d) $\frac{12}{17} = \frac{36}{\square}$

2 Change these improper fractions to mixed numbers. (4 marks)

a) $\frac{5}{2} =$ .... b) $\frac{5}{3} =$ .... c) $\frac{9}{2} =$ .... d) $\frac{12}{11} =$ ....

3 Work out the answers to the following. (8 marks)

a) $\frac{2}{9} + \frac{1}{3}$ .... b) $\frac{7}{11} - \frac{1}{4}$ .... c) $\frac{4}{7} \times \frac{3}{8}$ .... d) $\frac{9}{12} \div \frac{1}{4}$ ....

e) $\frac{5}{7} - \frac{1}{21}$ .... f) $\frac{4}{9} + \frac{3}{27}$ .... g) $\frac{7}{12} \times \frac{3}{2}$ .... h) $\frac{11}{7} \div \frac{12}{7}$ ....

4 Arrange these fractions in order of size, smallest first. (Hint: Change all fractions to fractions with same denominator.)

a) $\frac{2}{3}$ $\frac{4}{5}$ $\frac{1}{7}$ $\frac{3}{4}$ $\frac{1}{2}$ $\frac{3}{10}$ (2 marks)

....

b) $\frac{5}{8}$ $\frac{1}{3}$ $\frac{2}{7}$ $\frac{1}{9}$ $\frac{3}{4}$ $\frac{2}{5}$ (2 marks)

....

5 Decide whether these statements are true or false.

a) $\frac{4}{5}$ of 20 is bigger than $\frac{6}{7}$ of 14. .... (1 mark)

b) $\frac{2}{9}$ of 27 is smaller than $\frac{1}{3}$ of 15. .... (1 mark)

Score / 22

C **These are GCSE-style questions. Answer all parts of the questions. Show your workings (on separate paper if necessary) and include the correct units in your answers.**

1 **Gill says 'I've got three-fifths of a bottle of orange juice.'**

Jonathan says 'I've got two-thirds of a bottle of orange juice and my bottle of orange juice is the same size as yours.'

Who has got the most orange juice, Gill or Jonathan? Explain your answer. (2 marks)

....

....

2 **Work out these.**

a) $\frac{2}{3} + \frac{4}{5}$ .... (1 mark)

b) $\frac{9}{11} - \frac{1}{3}$ .... (1 mark)

c) $\frac{2}{7} \times \frac{4}{9}$ .... (1 mark)

d) $\frac{3}{10} \div \frac{2}{5}$ .... (1 mark)

3 **Charlotte's take-home pay is £930. She gives her mother $\frac{1}{3}$ of this and spends $\frac{1}{5}$ of the £930 on going out. What fraction of the £930 is left? Give your answer as a fraction in its lowest terms.** (3 marks)

....

....

4 **In a class of 32 pupils, $\frac{1}{8}$ are left-handed. How many students are not left-handed?** (1 mark)

....

5 **Thomas shares a bag of 30 sweets with his friends. He gives Jessica $\frac{2}{5}$ of his sweets, and gives Samuel $\frac{1}{6}$ of his sweets. He keeps the rest for himself. How many sweets does Thomas keep for himself?** (3 marks)

....

....

Score / 13

How well did you do? ✗ 1–11 Try again 12–21 Getting there 22–32 Good work 33–40 Excellent! ✓

For more information on this topic see pages 10–11 of your Success Guide.

Decimals

A

Choose just one answer, a, b, c or d.

1 **Here are some discs.**

5.8   5.79   5.81   5.805

Which of these discs has the largest number?

a) 5.8   b) 5.79   (1 mark)
c) 5.81   d) 5.805

2 **Work out the answer to 9.45 × 5**   (1 mark)

a) 47.52   b) 56.7
c) 47.25   d) 46.75

3 **If a piece of cheese weighs 0.3 kg, how much would 70 identical pieces of cheese weigh?**

a) 2.1 kg   b) 21 kg   (1 mark)
c) 0.21 kg   d) 210 kg

4 **Work out the answer to 520 ÷ 0.02**   (1 mark)

a) 2600   b) 260
c) 260000   d) 26000

5 **Round 18.629 to 2 decimal places**   (1 mark)

a) 18.69   b) 18.63
c) 18.7   d) 18.62

Score   / 5

B

Answer all parts of the questions.

1 **Look at these statements and decide whether they are true or false.**

a) 0.72 is bigger than 0.724. .... (1 mark)
b) 6.427 rounded to 2 decimal places is 6.43. .... (1 mark)
c) 12.204 is smaller than 12.214. .... (1 mark)
d) 37.465 rounded to 1 decimal place is 37.5. .... (1 mark)
e) 27.406 rounded to 2 decimal places is 27.41. .... (1 mark)

2 **Here are some number cards.** 7.32   7.09   8.31   8.315   7.102   7.321   (2 marks)

Arrange these number cards in order of size, smallest first. ....

3 **Four friends run a race. Their times in seconds are shown in the table below.**

Thomas	Hussain	Molly	Joshua
14.072	15.12	14.07	16.321

a) Who won the race? .... (1 mark)
b) What is the difference between Hussain and Joshua's times? .... (1 mark)
c) How much faster was Molly than Thomas? .... (1 mark)

4 **Here are some calculations. Fill in the gaps to make the statements correct.**   (6 marks)

a) 640 ÷ 40 = ...   b) 500 × 0.2 = ...   c) 600 ÷ 0.3 ....
d) 40 ÷ .... = 400   e) .... × 0.02 = 0.48   f) 420 ÷ .... = 42000

Score   / 16

C

These are GCSE-style questions. Answer all parts of the questions. Show your workings (on separate paper if necessary) and include the correct units in your answers.

1 Here are some number cards.

6.14	7.29	7.42	7.208	6.141

a) Arrange the cards in order of size, smallest first. (2 marks)

b) Work out the difference between the highest number and the smallest number. (1 mark)

....

c) What is the total of all of these cards? (1 mark)

....

d) Round these cards to 2 decimal places.

7.208	6.141

i) 7.208 becomes .... (1 mark)

ii) 6.141 becomes .... (1 mark)

2 Here are some number cards.

0.1	0.01	0.001	100	10

Use one of the number cards to fill each gaps to make the statements correct.

a) 60 ÷ .... = 6000 (1 mark)

b) 25 × .... = 2.5 (1 mark)

c) 720 ÷ .... = 720000 (1 mark)

3 a) Write the number 0.629 as a fraction. .... (1 mark)

b) Write $\frac{7}{25}$ as a decimal. .... (1 mark)

Score / 11

How well did you do? ✗ 1–7 Try again 8–15 Getting there 16–25 Good work 26–32 Excellent! ✓

For more information on this topic see pages 12–15 of your Success Guide.

Percentages 1

A

Choose just one answer, a, b, c or d.

1 Work out 10% of £850. (1 mark)

a) £8.50 b) £0.85
c) £85 d) £42.50

2 Work out 17.5% of £60. (1 mark)

a) £9
b) £15
c) £10.50
d) £12.50

3 In a survey, 17 people out of 25 said they preferred type A cola. What percentage of people preferred type A cola? (1 mark)

a) 68% b) 60%
c) 72% d) 75%

4 A CD player costs £45. In a sale the price is reduced by 20%. What is the sale price of the CD player? (1 mark)

a) £38
b) £40.50
c) £9
d) £36

5 A sofa costs £850. In a sale, it is reduced by 30%. What is the sale price of the sofa? (C) (1 mark)

a) £255
b) £765
c) £85
d) £595

Score /5

B

Answer all parts of the questions.

1 Draw a line from each calculation to the correct answer. (3 marks)

10% of 30	16
5% of 15	3
40% of 40	5
25% of 20	0.75

2 Last year Colin earned £25 500. This year he has a 3% pay rise. How much per year does Colin now earn? (C) (2 marks)

£ ....

3 A coat costs £120. In a sale it is reduced by 15%. Work out the sale price of the coat. (C) (2 marks)

....

4 Lucinda scored 58 out of 75 in a test. What percentage did she get? Give your answer to the nearest whole number. (C) (2 marks)

.... %

5 The cost of a parking ticket is £1.50. The price of the ticket rose by 20%. What is the cost of a parking ticket after the price increase? (C)

.... (2 marks)

6 12 out of 30 people wear glasses. What percentage wear glasses? (C) (2 marks)

.... %

Score /13

(C) *Indicates that a calculator may be used*

PERCENTAGES 1

Number

C

These are GCSE-style questions. Answer all parts of the questions. Show your workings (on separate paper if necessary) and include the correct units in your answers.

1 The price of a television set is £175 plus VAT. VAT is charged at a rate of 17.5%.

a) Work out the amount of VAT charged. (C) (2 marks)

....

b) In a sale, normal prices are reduced by 15%. The normal price of a washing machine is £399.

Work out the sale price of the washing machine. (3 marks)

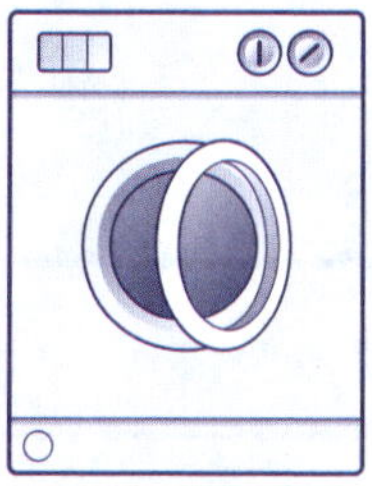

....

2 The price of a train ticket increases by 15%. The old price of the ticket was £26. Work out the new price of the ticket. (C) (3 marks)

.... %

3 Ruby sells some books. She sells each book for £7.80 plus VAT at 17.5%.
She sells 470 books.

Work out how much money Ruby receives. (C) (4 marks)

....

....

....

....

£ ....

Score / 12

How well did you do? ✗ 1–7 Try again 8–16 Getting there 17–23 Good work 24–30 Excellent! ✓

For more information on this topic see pages 16–17 of your Success Guide.

Percentages 2

A

Choose just one answer, a, b, c or d.

1 £2000 is invested in a savings account. Simple interest is paid at 2.1%. How much interest is paid after 1 year? (C) (1 mark)

a) £42
b) £5.20
c) £84.88
d) £84

2 A bike was bought for £120. Each year it depreciated by 10%. What was the bike worth 2 years later? (C) (1 mark)

a) £97.20
b) £98
c) £216
d) £110

3 Roberto has £5000 in his savings account. Simple interest is paid at 3%. How much does he have in his savings account at the end of the year? (C) (1 mark)

a) £4850
b) £5010
c) £5150
d) £5140.50

4 Lucy earns £23 500. National Insurance (NI) is deducted at 9%. How much NI must she pay?

a) £2250 (C) (1 mark)
b) £2115
c) £2200
d) £21 385

Score / 4

B

Answer all parts of the questions.

1 A meal costs £143. VAT at 17.5% is added to the price of the meal. What is the final price of the meal? (C) (2 marks)

£ ....

2 VAT of 5% is added to a gas bill of £72. Find the total amount to be paid. (C) (2 marks)

£ ....

3 A motorbike is bought for £9000. Each year it depreciates in value by 12%. Work out the value of the motorbike after 2 years. (C) (2 marks)

£ ....

4 A computer is bought for £799. Each year it depreciates in value by 30%. Work out the value of the computer after 2 years. (C) (2 marks)

£ ....

5 A house was bought for £112 000. After the first year the price had increased by 8%, during the second year it increased in price by a further 12%. What is the house now worth? (C) (2 marks)

£ ....

6 Petrol cost 113.2 pence per litre. The price increased by 2%. Six months later it increased again, by 5%. How much does a litre of petrol now cost? (C) (2 marks)

.... pence

Score / 12

(C) *Indicates that a calculator may be used*

C

These are GCSE-style questions. Answer all parts of the questions. Show your workings (on separate paper if necessary) and include the correct units in your answers.

1 a) **Work out 40% of £2500.** (2 marks)

....

b) **Find the simple interest on £2000 invested for 2 years at 4% per year.** (3 marks)

....

2 A year ago Matthew's height was 1.43 metres. His height has now increased by 12.3%.
Work out Matthew's height now. Give your answer to an appropriate degree of accuracy. (C) (3 marks)

....

3 Nigel opened an account at his local bank with £450. After one year, the bank paid him interest. He then had £465.75 in his account.

a) **Work out, as a percentage, his local bank's interest rate.** (C) (3 marks)

....

....

b) **Lucy opened a bank account. She invested £700 for 2 years at 4% simple interest. How much money did she have in her account after 2 years?** (3 marks)

....

....

4 Sara buys a car for £14000. Each year the value of the car depreciated by 10%. Work out the value of the car two years after she bought it. (3 marks)

....

....

Score / 17

How well did you do? ✗ 1–8 Try again 9–14 Getting there 15–24 Good work 25–33 Excellent! ✓

For more information on this topic see pages 16–19 of your Success Guide.

Fractions, decimals & percentages

A

Choose just one answer, a, b, c or d.

1 What is $\frac{3}{5}$ as a percentage? (1 mark)

a) 30% b) 25%
c) 60% d) 75%

2 What is $\frac{2}{3}$ written as a decimal? (1 mark)

a) 0.77 b) $0.\dot{6}$
c) 0.665 d) 0.6

3 What is the smallest value in this list?
29%, 0.4, $\frac{3}{4}$, $\frac{1}{8}$ (1 mark)

a) 29% b) 0.4 c) $\frac{3}{4}$ d) $\frac{1}{8}$

4 What is the largest value in this list?
$\frac{4}{5}$, 80%, $\frac{2}{3}$, 0.9 (1 mark)

a) $\frac{4}{5}$ b) 80%
c) $\frac{2}{3}$ d) 0.9

5 Change $\frac{5}{8}$ into a decimal. (1 mark)

a) 0.625 b) 0.425
c) 0.125 d) 0.725

Score / 5

B

Answer all parts of the questions.

1 The table shows equivalent fractions, decimals and percentages. Fill in the gaps. (6 marks)

Fraction	Decimal	Percentage
$\frac{2}{5}$		
		5%
	$0.\dot{3}$	
	0.04	
		25%
$\frac{1}{8}$		

2 Put these cards in order of size, smallest first. (2 marks)

0.37 | 30% | $\frac{3}{8}$ | $\frac{1}{3}$ | 92% | $\frac{1}{2}$ | 0.62

....

3 A sundial is being sold in two different garden centres. The cost of the sundial is £89.99 in both garden centres. Both garden centres have a promotion.

Gardens are Us: **Sundial 22% off**

Rosebushes: **Sundial $\frac{1}{4}$ off**

In which garden centre is the sundial the cheapest? Explain your reasoning. (2 marks)

....

....

Score / 10

Ⓒ *Indicates that a calculator may be used*

C

These are GCSE-style questions. Answer all parts of the questions. Show your workings (on separate paper if necessary) and include the correct units in your answers.

1 **Write this list of seven numbers in order of size. Start with the smallest number.** (3 marks)

25% $\frac{1}{3}$ 0.27 $\frac{2}{5}$ 0.571 72% $\frac{1}{8}$

....

2 **Philippa is buying a new television. She sees three different advertisements for the same television set.**

Ed's Electricals
TV normal price
£250
Sale 10% off

Sheila's Bargains
TV £185 plus
VAT at $17\frac{1}{2}$%

GITA's TV SHOP
Normal price
£290
Sale: $\frac{1}{5}$ off normal price

Find the maximum and minimum prices that Philippa could pay for the television set. (C) (7 marks)

Maximum price = ...

Minimum price = ...

3 **Decide whether these calculations give the same answer for this question:** (C) (2 marks)

Increase £40 by 20%

Jack says:

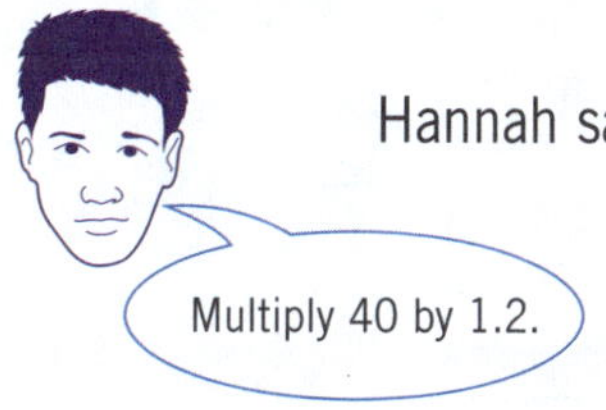

Hannah says:

....

4 **Place these fractions in order of size, smallest first** (2 marks)

$\frac{2}{3}, \frac{1}{10}, \frac{5}{8}, \frac{3}{5}, \frac{9}{10}$ ....

Score / 14

How well did you do? ✗ 1–7 Try again 8–13 Getting there 14–22 Good work 23–29 Excellent! ✓

For more information on this topic see pages 16–20 of your Success Guide.

Approximations & using a calculator

A Choose just one answer, a, b, c or d.

1 Estimate the answer to the calculation
27×41 (1 mark)

a) 1107   b) 1200
c) 820   d) 1300

2 A carton of orange juice costs 79p. Estimate the cost of 402 cartons of orange juice. (1 mark)

a) £350   b) £250
c) £400   d) £320

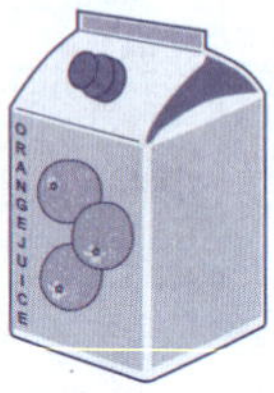

3 A school trip is organised. 396 pupils are going on the trip. Each coach seats 50 pupils. Approximately how many coaches are needed?

a) 12   b) 5 (1 mark)
c) 8   d) 10

4 Estimate the answer to the calculation
$\frac{(4.2)^2}{107}$ (1 mark)

a) 16   b) 1.6
c) 0.16   d) 160

5 Round 5379 to 3 significant figures.

a) 538   b) 5370 (1 mark)
c) 537   d) 5380

Score /5

B Answer all parts of the questions.

1 Decide whether each statement is true or false. (4 marks)

a) 2.742 rounded to 3 significant figures is 2.74. ....

b) 2793 rounded to 2 significant figures is 27. ....

c) 32 046 rounded to 1 significant figure is 40 000. ....

d) 14.637 rounded to 3 significant figures is 14.6. ....

2 Round each of the numbers in these calculations to 1 significant figure and work out an approximate answer. (2 marks)

a) $\frac{(32.9)^2}{9.1}$ ....   b) $\frac{(906 \div 31.4)^2}{7.1 + 2.9}$ ....

3 Work these out on your calculator. Give your answers to 3 s.f. (C) (3 marks)

a) $\frac{4.2(3.6 + 5.1)}{2 - 1.9}$ ....   b) $6 \times \sqrt{\frac{12.1}{4.2}}$ ....

c) $\frac{12^5}{4.3 \times 9.15}$ ....

4 James has 6^{09} on his calculator display. What does this mean? (2 marks)

....

5 3×10^2 is the same as 300. True or false? .... (1 mark)

Score /12

(C) *Indicates that a calculator may be used*

C

These are GCSE-style questions. Answer all parts of the questions. Show your workings (on separate paper if necessary) and include the correct units in your answers.

1 a) Write down two numbers you could use to get an approximate answer to this question. (1 mark)

31×79 .... and ....

b) Work out your approximate answer. (1 mark)

....

c) Work out the difference between your approximate answer and the exact answer. (2 marks)

....

2 Use your calculator to work out the value of the calculation below. Give your answer correct to 3 significant figures. (C)

$$\frac{\sqrt{4.9^2 + 6.3}}{2.1 \times 0.37}$$

(3 marks)

....

3 a) Use your calculator to work out the value of this expression. Write down all the figures on your calculator display. (C) (2 marks)

$$\frac{27.1 \times 6.2}{38.2 - 9.9}$$

....

b) Round each of the numbers in the above calculation to 1 significant figure and obtain an approximate answer. (3 marks)

....

4 Estimate the answer to the following. Leave your answer as an improper fraction in its simplest form. (3 marks)

$$\frac{21.2^2 - 10.3^2}{3.6 \times 29}$$

....

5 a) Use your calculator to work out the value of the following. Write down all the figures on your calculator display. (2 marks)

$$\frac{(15.2 + 6.9)^2}{3.63 - 4.2}$$

....

b) Round your answer to 3 significant figures. .... (1 mark)

Score / 18

How well did you do? 1–10 Try again 11–17 Getting there 18–24 Good work 25–35 Excellent!

For more information on this topic see pages 14–15 & 21–23 of your Success Guide.

Ratio

A Choose just one answer, a, b, c or d.

1 What is the ratio 6 : 18 written in its simplest form? (1 mark)

a) 3 : 1 b) 3 : 9
c) 1 : 3 d) 9 : 3

2 Write the ratio 200 : 500 in the form 1 : *n*.

a) 1 : 50 b) 1 : 5 (1 mark)
c) 1 : 25 d) 1 : 2.5

3 If £140 is divided in the ratio 3 : 4, what is the size of the larger share? (1 mark)

a) £45 b) £60
c) £80 d) £90

4 A recipe for 4 people needs 800 g of flour. How much flour is needed for 6 people? (1 mark)

a) 12 g b) 120 g
c) 12 kg d) 1200 g

5 If 9 oranges cost £1.08, how much would 14 similar oranges cost? (1 mark)

a) £1.50 b) £1.68
c) £1.20 d) £1.84

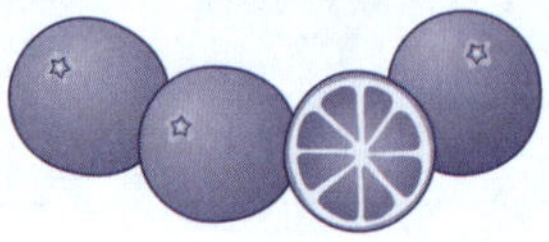

Score / 5

B Answer all parts of the questions.

1 Write down each of the following ratios in the form 1 : *n*.

a) 10 : 15 .... (1 mark)
b) 6 : 10 .... (1 mark)
c) 9 : 27 .... (1 mark)

2 Seven bottles of lemonade have a total capacity of 1680 ml. Work out the total capacity of five similar bottles. (1 mark)

....

3 a) Increase £4.10 in the ratio 2 : 5 .... (1 mark)

b) Decrease 120 g in the ratio 5 : 2 .... (1 mark)

4 Mrs London inherited £55 000. She divided the money between her children in the ratio 3 : 3 : 5. How much did the child with the largest share receive? (2 marks)

£ ....

5 It takes 6 men 3 days to dig and lay a cable. How long would it take 4 men? (All the men work at the same rate.) (2 marks)

.... days

Score / 10

RATIO

Number

C

These are GCSE-style questions. Answer all parts of the questions. Show your workings (on separate paper if necessary) and include the correct units in your answers.

1 7 metre of rope costs £5.46. Work out the cost of 13 metre of the same rope. (2 marks)

....

2 Vicky and Tracy share £14 400 in the ratio 4 : 5. Work out how much each of them receives. (3 marks)

Vicky £ .... Tracy £ ....

3 James uses these ingredients to make 12 buns.

50 g butter
40 g sugar
2 eggs
45 g flour
15 ml milk

James wants to make 30 similar buns. Write down how much of each ingredient he needs for 30 buns. (3 marks)

butter .... g sugar .... g

eggs .... flour .... g

milk .... ml

4 It takes 3 builders 16 days to build a wall. All the builders work at the same rate. How long would it take 8 builders to build a wall the same size? (3 marks)

....

5 Mineral water is sold in two sizes.

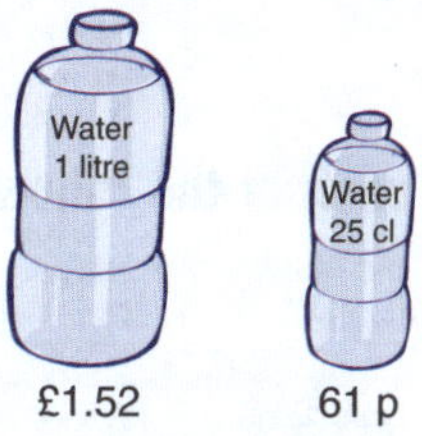

Which size bottle gives the better value for money? You must show all of your working. (2 marks)

....

....

Score / 13

How well did you do? ✗ 1–6 Try again 7–12 Getting there 13–20 Good work 21–28 Excellent! ✓

For more information on this topic see pages 24–25 of your Success Guide.

Indices

A

Choose just one answer, a, b, c or d.

1 In index form, what is the value of $8^3 \times 8^{11}$? (1 mark)

a) 8^{14} b) 8^{33}
c) 64^{14} d) 64^{33}

2 In index form, what is the value of $4^2 \times 4^3$? (1 mark)

a) 12^2 b) 4^5
c) 4^6 d) 16^6

3 What is the value of $5^2 \times 2^2$? (1 mark)

a) 40 b) 50
c) 25 d) 100

4 What is the value of $2^3 \times 3^2$? (1 mark)

a) 36 b) 54
c) 48 d) 72

5 What is the value of $7^{12} \div 7^2$ written in index form? (1 mark)

a) 7^{10} b) 7^6
c) 7^{14} d) 7^{24}

Score / 5

B

Answer all parts of the questions.

1 Work out the exact value of these. (3 marks)

a) 4^3 .... b) 2^5 .... c) 3^4 ....

2 Decide whether each of these expressions is true or false. (6 marks)

a) $a^4 \times a^5 = a^{20}$ ....
b) $2a^4 \times 3a^2 = 5a^8$ ....
c) $10a^6 \div 2a^4 = 5a^2$ ....
d) $20a^4b^2 \div 10a^5b = \frac{2b}{a}$ ....
e) $7^3 \times 7^4 = 7^{12}$ ....
f) $4^1 = 4$ ....

3 Simplify the following expressions. (8 marks)

a) $3a \times 2a =$ ....
b) $12m^3 \div 4m =$ ....
c) $10a^2b^4 \times 2ab =$ ....
d) $n^7 \times n^9 =$ ....
e) $a^2 \times a^4 =$ ....
f) $12a^4 \div 16a^7 =$ ....
g) $4a^5 \times 3a^6 =$ ....
h) $12b^3 \div 4b =$ ....

4 Find the value of n in each of the following equations. (3 marks)

a) $8^{10} \times 8^n = 8^{16}$ ....
b) $10^n \div 10^{-2} = 10^{12}$ ....
c) $5^n = 5$ ....

Score / 20

Ⓒ *Indicates that a calculator may be used*

C

These are GCSE-style questions. Answer all parts of the questions. Show your workings (on separate paper if necessary) and include the correct units in your answers.

1 a) Work out the value of the following. (3 marks)

i) 4^2 ....

ii) 3^3 ....

b) Write as a power of 9:

$9 \times 9 \times 9 \times 9 \times 9$ ....

2 Simplify the following. (4 marks)

a) $p^3 \times p^4$ ....

b) $\frac{n^7}{n^3}$ ....

c) $\frac{a^3 \times a^4}{a}$ ....

d) $\frac{12a^2b}{3a}$ ....

3 Work out the value of the following. (C) (3 marks)

a) 3^1 ....

b) 5^2 ....

c) $3^4 \times 2^3$ ....

4 a) Evaluate the following. (3 marks)

i) 8^1 ....

ii) 6^2 ....

iii) $2^3 \times 2^2$ ....

b) Write this expression as a single power of 5. (2 marks)

$\frac{5^7 \times 5^3}{5^6}$ ....

5 Simplify the following. (3 marks)

a) $2a^3 \times 3a^2$ ....

b) $\frac{12a^2b}{4ab}$ ....

c) $\frac{b^6 \times 3b^2}{12b^{10}}$ ....

6 Evaluate the following. (3 marks)

a) i) 7^2 .... ii) $3^2 \times 3^3$ .... iii) $4^7 \div 4^5$ ....

b) Write $\frac{3^4 \times 3^6}{3^2}$ as a single power of 3. .... (2 marks)

Score / 23

How well did you do? ✗ 1–12 Try again 13–24 Getting there 25–37 Good work 38–48 Excellent! ✓

For more information on this topic see pages 26–27 of your Success Guide.

Algebra 1

A

Choose just one answer, a, b, c or d.

1 There are n books in a pile. Each book is 5 cm thick. What is the formula for the total height h of the pile of books? (1 mark)

a) $5n$ b) $h = 5n$
c) $h = \frac{n}{5}$ d) $h = \frac{5}{n}$

2 What is the expression $4a + 3b - a + 6b$ when it is fully simplified? (1 mark)

a) $9b - 3a$ b) $3a9b$
c) $3a + 9b$ d) $5a + 9b$

3 What is the expression $7a - 4b + 6a - 3b$ when it is fully simplified? (1 mark)

a) $7b - a$ b) $13a + 7b$
c) $a - 7b$ d) $13a - 7b$

4 If $a = \frac{b}{c}$ and $b = 12$ and $c = 4$, what is the value of a? (1 mark)

a) 12 b) 4
c) 6 d) 3

5 If $m = \sqrt{\frac{r^2p}{4}}$ $r = 3$ and $p = 6$, what is the value of m to 1 decimal place? Ⓒ (1 mark)

a) 13.5 b) 182.3
c) 3.7 d) 3

Score /5

B

Answer all parts of the questions.

1 Decide whether these simplified expressions are true or false.

a) $3a - 2b + 5a + b = 8a - b$ .... (1 mark)

b) $6ay - 3ay^2 + 2ay^2 - 4ay = 2ay - ay^2$ .... (1 mark)

c) $3ab + 2a^2b - a^2b + 4ba = a^2b + 12a^2 + b^2$ .... (1 mark)

2 John buys b books costing £6 each and m magazines costing 67 pence each.

Write down a formula for the total cost (T) of the books and magazines. (2 marks)

$T =$ ....

3 $a = \frac{b^2 + 2c}{4}$

a) Calculate a if $b = 2$ and $c = 6$. .... Ⓒ (1 mark)

b) Calculate a if $b = 3$ and $c = -2$. .... Ⓒ (1 mark)

c) Calculate b if $a = 25$ and $c = 18$. .... Ⓒ (1 mark)

Score /8

Ⓒ *Indicates that a calculator may be used*

C

These are GCSE-style questions. Answer all parts of the questions. Show your workings (on separate paper if necessary) and include the correct units in your answers.

1 Here is a table for a two stage number machine.
It multiplies by 4 and subtracts 2.
Complete the missing numbers in the table. **(3 marks)**

$\times 4 - 2$	
Input	Output
1	2
2	6
4	....
6	....
....	34

2 a) Simplify: $t + t$ .... **(1 mark)**

b) Simplify: $y^2 + y^2 + y^2$ .... **(1 mark)**

3 a) Simplify fully: $7n - 4n + 3n$ .... **(1 mark)**

b) Simplify fully: $3a \times 2b$ .... **(1 mark)**

4 a) Using algebra, write in symbols the rule 'To find p, multiply n by 5 and then subtract 6.' **(1 mark)**

....

b) Work out the value of p when $n = -2$. **(1 mark)**

....

5 Peter uses this formula to calculate the value of V.

$$V = \frac{x(2R^2 + t^2)}{500}$$

$$x = 20, \quad R = 5, \quad t = -4$$

Calculate the value of V. (C) **(3 marks)**

$V =$ ....

6 Charlotte is given a formula in Physics: $v^2 = u^2 + 2as$

Charlotte works out the answer where $u = -5$, $a = 10$, $s = 2$.

She writes $v^2 = -5^2 + 2 \times 10 \times 2$
$v^2 = 25 + 40$
$v = 65$

Explain what Charlotte has done wrong. (C) .... **(2 marks)**

....

Score / 14

How well did you do? ✗ 1–5 Try again 6–11 Getting there 12–19 Good work 20–27 Excellent! ✓

For more information on this topic see pages 30–32 of your Success Guide.

Algebra 2

A

Choose just one answer, a, b, c or d.

1 What is the expression $3(2x - 1)$ when it is multiplied out and simplified? (1 mark)

a) $6x - 3$ b) $6x - 1$
c) $2x - 3$ d) $6x + 3$

2 Factorise fully the expression $25x + 15$ (1 mark)

a) $5(5x + 15)$ b) $25(x + 15)$
c) $5(5x + 3)$ d) $5(5x)$

3 What is $(n - 3)^2$ when it is multiplied out and simplified? (1 mark)

a) $n^2 + 9$ b) $n^2 + 6n - 9$
c) $n^2 - 6n - 9$ d) $n^2 - 6n + 9$

4 Rearrange the formula $a = b + 4c$ to make c the subject. (1 mark)

a) $c = \frac{a+b}{4}$ b) $c = a + 4b$
c) $c = \frac{a-b}{4}$ d) $c = 4b + a$

5 Rearrange the formula $P = 5a + b$ to make a the subject. (1 mark)

a) $a = \frac{P-b}{5}$ b) $a = \frac{P+b}{5}$
c) $a = 5P + b$ d) $a = 5P - b$

Score / 5

B

Answer all parts of the questions.

1 Some expressions are written on cards. Choose one expression and copy it in each space to make each statement correct. (4 marks)

$3n - 3$	$8(n + 2)$	$n^2 - 3n + 2$	$n^2 + 2$	$5(n + 3)$	$3n - 9$

a) $3(n - 3) =$ .... b) $5n + 15 =$ ....
c) $(n - 1)(n - 2) =$ .... d) $8n + 16 =$ ....

2 Factorise the following expressions. (5 marks)

a) $10n + 15$ .... b) $24 - 36n$ ....
c) $5 + 10n$ .... d) $20 - 4n$ ....
e) $6a^2 + 12a$ ....

3 Rearrange each of the formulae below to make b the subject.

a) $p = 3b - 4$ .... (1 mark)
b) $y = \frac{ab - 6}{4}$ .... (1 mark)
c) $5(n + b) = 2b + 2$ .... (1 mark)

4 $F = ma$ is a formula. True or false? .... (1 mark)

Score / 13

C

These are GCSE-style questions. Answer all parts of the questions. Show your workings (on separate paper if necessary) and include the correct units in your answers.

1 a) Expand and simplify $6x - 2(x - 2)$ (2 marks)

....

b) (i) Factorise $6a + 12$ .... (1 mark)

(ii) Factorise completely $10a^2 - 15ab$ .... (2 marks)

2 In each of these questions, make x the subject of the formula.

a) $p = 5x - 2y$ (3 marks) b) $2(p + x) = 3x - 2$ (3 marks)

....

....

3 Show that $n(n + 2) - 3(n - 1)$ simplifies to $n^2 - n + 3$ (3 marks)

....

....

....

4 a) Expand and simplify $2(3a - 1) - (a - 2)$ (2 marks)

....

b) Factorise fully the following expressions. (2 marks)

(i) $3n - 12$ ....

(ii) $8pq - 12p$ ....

5 a) Make h the subject of the formula $a = b + 5h$ (2 marks)

....

....

b) If $b = 4$ and $h = -2$ work out the value of a. (2 marks)

....

....

c) Expand and simplify.

i) $3(n + 4) + 2(n - 1)$ (2 marks)

....

....

ii) $5(2n - 1) - 3(n + 2)$ (3 marks)

....

....

Score / 27

How well did you do? 1–12 Try again 13–23 Getting there 24–34 Good work 35–45 Excellent!

For more information on this topic see pages 32–33 of your Success Guide.

Equations 1

A

Choose just one answer, a, b, c or d.

1 **Solve the equation $4n - 2 = 10$** (1 mark)

a) $n = 4$ b) $n = 2$
c) $n = 3$ d) $n = 3.5$

2 **Solve the equation $\frac{n}{2} + 4 = 2$** (1 mark)

a) $n = -4$ b) $n = 4$
c) $n = 12$ d) $n = -12$

3 **Solve the equation $4(x + 3) = 16$** (1 mark)

a) $x = 9$ b) $x = 7$
c) $x = 4$ d) $x = 1$

4 **Solve the equation $4(n + 2) = 8(n - 3)$** (1 mark)

a) $n = 16$
b) $n = 8$
c) $n = 4$
d) $n = 12$

5 **Solve the equation $10 - 6n = 4n - 5$** (1 mark)

a) $n = 2$
b) $n = -2$
c) $n = 1.5$
d) $n = -1.5$

Score / 5

B

Answer all parts of the questions.

1 **Solve the following equations.** (6 marks)

a) $n - 3 = 6$ ....
b) $n + 10 = 12$ ....
c) $3n - 1 = 5$ ....
d) $5 - n = 12$ ....
e) $\frac{n}{6} = 3$ ....
f) $5n + 1 = 6$ ....

2 Reece thinks of a number. (2 marks)
He adds 4 to the number.
He then multiplies by 5.
His answer is 25.
What number did Reece think of ?

....

3 **Solve the following equations.** (6 marks)

a) $5n = 25$ ....
b) $\frac{36}{n} = 12$ ....
c) $2n - 4 = 10$ ....
d) $3 - 2n = 14$ ....
e) $\frac{n}{5} + 2 = 7$ ....
f) $4 - \frac{n}{2} = 2$ ....

4 **Solve the following equations.** (4 marks)

a) $12n + 5 = 3n + 32$ ....
b) $5n - 4 = 3n + 6$ ....
c) $5(n + 1) = 25$ ....
d) $4(n - 2) = 3(n + 2)$ ....

Score / 18

C

These are GCSE-style questions. Answer all parts of the questions. Show your workings (on separate paper if necessary) and include the correct units in your answers.

1 **Solve these equations.**

a) $3n = 12$ (2 marks)

b) $5n + 3 = 18$ (3 marks)

c) $3(n + 2) = 21$ (3 marks)

d) $\frac{n-2}{4} = 3$ (2 marks)

2 **Solve these equations.**

a) $5m - 3 = 12$ (2 marks)

b) $8p + 3 = 9 - 2p$ (2 marks)

c) $5(x - 1) = 3x + 7$ (2 marks)

d) $4 + x = 2(x - 1)$ (2 marks)

3 **Solve these equations.**

a) $x - 4 = 12$ (1 mark)

b) $2x - 8 = 12$ (2 marks)

c) $5(x - 2) = 25$ (3 marks)

d) $7x + 4 = 4x - 5$ (3 marks)

4 a) **Sophie thinks of a number.**
She adds 9 to the number.
She then multiplies the result by 4.
Her answer is 60.

What number did Sophie first think of? (2 marks)

b) **Solve** $8 - 2x = 3x + 3$ (3 marks)

Score / 32

How well did you do? 0–18 Try again 19–29 Getting there 30–44 Good work 45–55 Excellent!

For more information on this topic see pages 34–36 of your Success Guide.

Equations 2 & inequalities

A

Choose just one answer, a, b, c or d.

1 $-4 \leq y < 2$

y is an integer. What are all the possible values of y? (1 mark)

a) −4, −3, −2, −1, 0, 1, 2
b) −3, −2, −1, 0, 1, 2
c) −4, −3, −2, −1, 0, 1
d) −3, −2, −1, 0, 1, 2

2 $-6 \leq 2n < 2$

n is an integer. What are all the possible values of n? (1 mark)

a) −6, −5, −4, −3, −2, −1, 0, 1
b) −3, −2, −1, 0, 1
c) −3, −2, −1, 0
d) −2, −1, 0, 1, 2

3 The equation $y^3 + 2y = 82$ has a solution between 4 and 5. By using a method of trial and improvement, find the solution to 1 decimal place. (C) (1 mark)

a) 3.9 b) 4.1
c) 4.2 d) 4.3

4 Solve the inequality $3x + 1 < 19$ (1 mark)

a) $x < 3$ b) $x < 7$
c) $x < 5$ d) $x < 6$

5 Solve the inequality $2x - 7 < 9$ (1 mark)

a) $x < 9$ b) $x < 10$
c) $x < 8$ d) $x < 6.5$

Score / 5

B

Answer all parts of the questions.

1 Use a trial and improvement method to solve the following equation. Give your answer to 1 decimal place. (C) (2 marks)

$t^2 - 2t = 20$ $t =$ ....

2 Solve the following inequalities.

a) $5x + 2 < 12$ (1 mark) ....

b) $\frac{x}{3} + 1 \geq 3$ (1 mark) ....

c) $3 \leq 2x + 1 \leq 9$ (1 mark) ....

d) $3 \leq 3x + 2 \leq 8$ (1 mark) ....

3 The angles in a triangle add up to 180°. Form an equation in n and solve it. (2 marks)

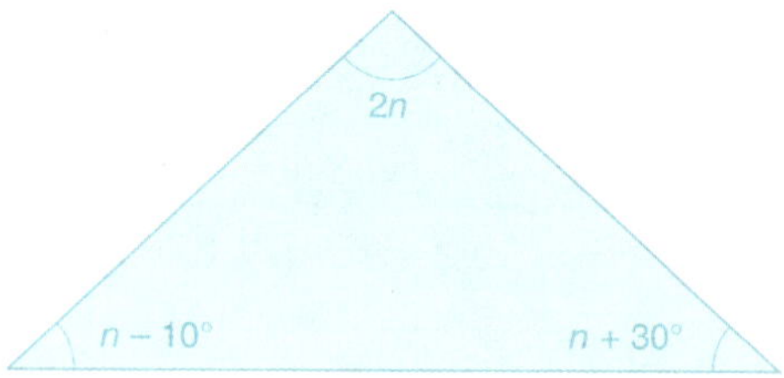

$n =$ ....

Score / 8

(C) Indicates that a calculator may be used

C

These are GCSE-style questions. Answer all parts of the questions. Show your workings (on separate paper if necessary) and include the correct units in your answers.

1 n is an integer.

a) Write down the values of n which satisfy the inequality $-4 < n \leq 2$ (2 marks)

....

b) Solve the inequality $5p - 2 \leq 8$ (2 marks)

....

2 Use the method of trial and improvement to solve the equation $x^3 + 3x = 28$. Give your answer correct to one decimal place. (C) You must show all your working. (4 marks)

....

....

....

$x =$ ....

3 The lengths, in cm, of the sides of the triangle are $2x + 2$, $2x - 1$, $5x + 3$.

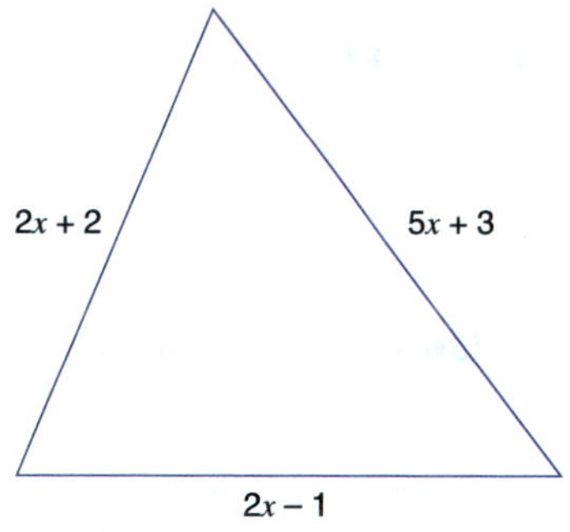

a) Write down, in terms of x, an expression for the perimeter of the triangle. (2 marks)

Give your expression in its simplest form.

....

....

b) The perimeter of the triangle is 22 cm. Work out the length of the shortest side of the triangle. (2 marks)

....

....

4 The equation $x^3 + 10x = 51$ has a solution between 2 and 3. (C)

Use a trial and improvement method to find this solution.
Give your answer correct to 1 decimal place.
You must show *all* your working. (4 marks)

....

....

$x =$ ....

Score / 16

How well did you do? ✗ 1–6 Try again 7–14 Getting there 15–22 Good work 23–29 Excellent! ✓

For more information on this topic see pages 36–39 of your Success Guide.

Number patterns and sequences

A

Choose just one answer, a, b, c or d.

1 Here are the first four terms in a sequence:
1, 4, 9, 16
What is the next number in the sequence? (1 mark)

a) 24 b) 49 c) 36 d) 25

2 What is the nth term of a sequence whose first four terms are 5, 7, 9, 11? (1 mark)

a) $2n + 3$ b) $2n - 3$
c) $n + 2$ d) $3 - 2n$

3 If the nth term of a sequence is given by $4 - 3n$, what is the fifth term of this sequence? (1 mark)

a) -8 b) -2 c) -11 d) -14

4 What is the nth term of a sequence whose first four terms are 18, 16, 14, 12? (1 mark)

a) $2n - 20$ b) $20 - 2n$
c) $n - 2$ d) $2n + 20$

Score / 4

B

Answer all parts of the questions.

1 Write down the next two terms in each of the sequences below. (4 marks)

a) 2, 4, 6, 8, ..., ...
b) 4, 7, 10, 13, ..., ...
c) 7, 17, 27, 37, ..., ...
d) 12, 6, 3, 1.5, ..., ...

2 The clouds below have some names of sequences. (3 marks)

even numbers
square numbers
powers of 10
triangular numbers
cube numbers

Match these sequences with the correct name.

a) 2, 4, 6, 8, 10 ....
b) 10, 100, 1000, 10000 ....
c) 1, 8, 27, 64 ....

3 Look at this sequence: 7, 10, 13, 16, . . .

a) What is the sixth number of this sequence? .... (1 mark)
b) Write down the nth term of this sequence. .... (1 mark)

4 Decide whether the nth term given is true or false for each of these sequences.

a) 1, 4, 7, 10, 13 nth term: $n + 3$ .... (1 mark)
b) 10, 6, 2, −2, −6 nth term: $10 - 4n$ .... (1 mark)
c) 1, 4, 7, 10 nth term: $3n - 2$ .... (1 mark)

5 Represent $-1 \leq n < 5$ on a number line .... (1 mark)

6 Solve the inequality $2x - 1 < 7$ .... (1 mark)

Score / 14

C

These are GCSE-style questions. Answer all parts of the questions. Show your workings (on separate paper if necessary) and include the correct units in your answers.

1 Here are some patterns made up of dots.

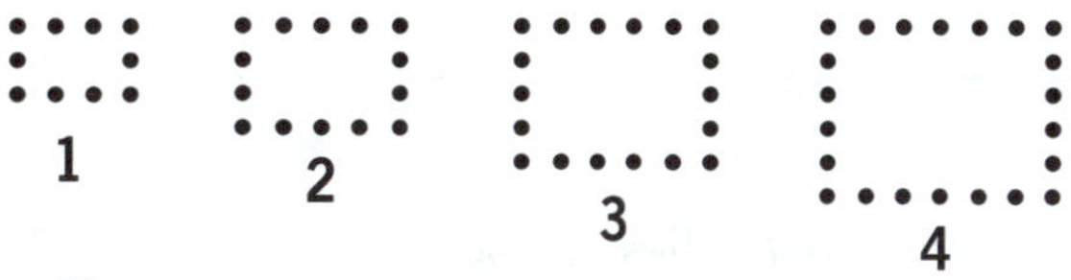

a) In the space below, draw pattern number 5. (1 mark)

b) Complete the table (1 mark)

Pattern number	1	2	3	4	5	6
Number of dots	10	14	18	22		

c) How many dots are used in pattern number 12? .... (1 mark)

2 Here are the first four numbers of a simple sequence.

5, 7, 9, 11

a) Write down the next two numbers of the sequence. .... (2 marks)

b) Write down in words, the rule to continue this sequence. (1 mark)

....

3 a) Here are the first five terms of a sequence.

64, 32, 16, 8, 4

Write down the next three terms in the sequence. ...., ..., ... (3 marks)

b) Here are the first five terms of a different sequence.

2, 7, 12, 17, 22

Find, in terms of n, an expression for the nth term for this sequence. (2 marks)

4 Here are the first four numbers in a sequence.

3, 7, 11, 15, . . .

Write down, in terms of n, the nth term for this sequence. (2 marks)

....

5 n is a whole number such that $8 \le 4n < 16$.

List all the possible values of n .... (3 marks)

Score / 16

How well did you do? ✗ 1–5 Try again 6–14 Getting there 15–25 Good work 26–34 Excellent! ✓

For more information on this topic see page 38–39 of your Success Guide.

Straight line graphs

A Choose just one answer, a, b, c or d.

1 Which pair of coordinates lies on the line $x = 2$? (1 mark)

a) (1, 3) b) (2, 3)
c) (3, 2) d) (0, 2)

2 Which pair of coordinates lies on the line $y = -3$? (1 mark)

a) (−3, 5) b) (5, −2)
c) (−2, 5) d) (5, −3)

3 What is the gradient of the line $y = 2 - 5x$? (1 mark)

a) −2 b) −5 c) 2 d) 5

4 These graphs have been drawn: $y = 3x - 1$, $y = 5 - 2x$, $y = 6x + 1$, $y = 2x - 3$. Which graph is the steepest? (1 mark)

a) $y = 3x - 1$
b) $y = 5 - 2x$
c) $y = 6x + 1$
d) $y = 2x - 3$

5 At what point does the graph $y = 3x - 4$ intercept the y axis? (1 mark)

a) (0, −4) b) (0, 3)
c) (−4, 0) d) (3, 0)

Score / 5

B Answer all parts of the questions.

1 a) Complete the table of values for $y = 6 - x$. (2 marks)

x	−2	−1	0	1	2
$y = 6 - x$			6		4

On the grid below, plot your values for x and y. Join your points with a straight line. (1 mark)

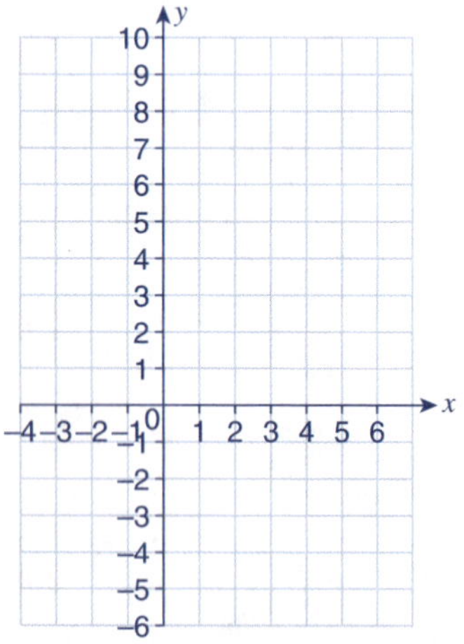

b) A second line goes through the coordinates (1, 5), (−2, −4) and (2, 8)

i) Draw this line. (1 mark)

ii) Write down the equation of the line you have just drawn. (2 marks)

....

c) What are the coordinates of the point where the two lines meet? (1 mark)

....

2 The equations of five straight lines are: $y = 2x - 4$, $y = 3 - 2x$, $y = 4 - 2x$, $y = 5x - 4$, $y = 3x - 5$. Two of the lines are parallel. Write down the equations of these two lines. (2 marks)

.... and ....

Score / 9

C

This is a GCSE-style questions. Answer all parts of the question. Show your workings (on separate paper if necessary) and include the correct units in your answers.

1 The line with equation $x + y = 4$ has been drawn on the grid.

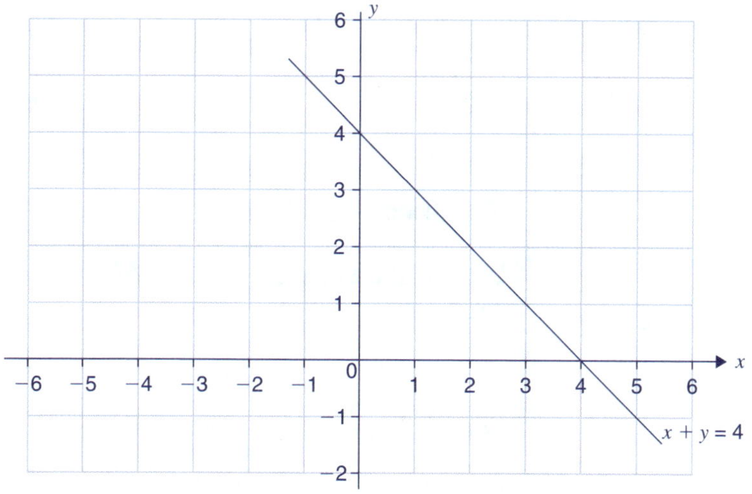

a) Write down the gradient of the line $x + y = 4$. (3 marks)

....

b) On the grid above draw the graph with the equation $y = 2x - 2$. (3 marks)

c) Write down the coordinates of the point of intersection of the two straight-line graphs. (1 mark)

(.................., ...)

d) Using the graph of $y = 2x - 2$ find the value of x when $y = 3$ (1 mark)

2 a) Write down an equation of a straight line that is parallel to the line $y = 2x$. (1 mark)

....

b) Are the lines $y = 3x - 2$ and $y = 4x + 1$ parallel? Give a reason for your answer. (1 mark)

....

Score /10

How well did you do? 1–4 Try again 5–9 Getting there 10–16 Good work 17–24 Excellent!

For more information on this topic see pages 40–41 of your Success Guide.

Curved graphs

A Choose just one answer, a, b, c or d.

1 **Which pair of coordinates lies on the graph $y = x^2 - 2$?** (1 mark)

a) (1, 1)
b) (4, 14)
c) (2, 4)
d) (0, 2)

2 **On which of these curves do the coordinates (2, 5) lie?** (1 mark)

a) $y = x^2 - 4$
b) $y = 2x^2 + 3$
c) $y = x^2 - 6$
d) $y = 2x^2 - 3$

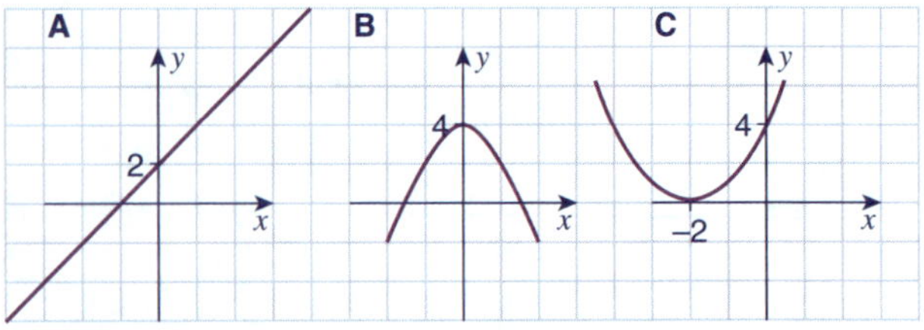

Questions 3–5 refer to these diagrams above.

3 **What is the equation of graph A?** (1 mark)

a) $y = 5 - 2x^2$ b) $y = x^2 + 4x + 4$
c) $y = x + 2$ d) $y = 4 - x^2$

4 **What is the equation of graph B?** (1 mark)

a) $y = 5 - 2x^2$ b) $y = x^2 + 4x + 4$
c) $y = x + 2$ d) $y = 4 - x^2$

5 **What is the equation of graph C?** (1 mark)

a) $y = 5 - 2x^2$ b) $y = x^2 + 4x + 4$
c) $y = x + 2$ d) $y = 4 - x^2$

Score / 5

B Answer all parts of the questions.

1 **a) Complete the table of values for $y = x^2 - 2x - 2$** (2 marks)

x	−2	−1	0	1	2	3
$y = x^2 - 2x - 2$			−2			1

b) On the grid below draw the graph of $y = x^2 - 2x - 2$ (3 marks)

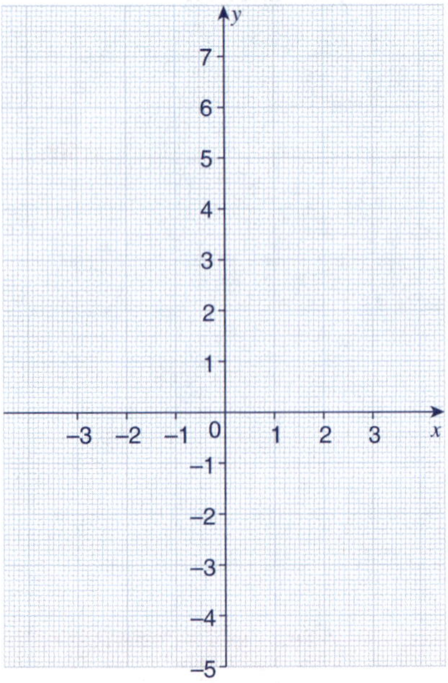

c) Use your graph to write down an estimate for:

i) the solutions of the equation $x^2 - 2x - 2 = -2$

y = ... (2 marks)

ii) the solutions of the equation $x^2 - 2x - 2 = 0$

x = ... and x = ... (2 marks)

Score / 9

C

These are GCSE-style questions. Answer all parts of the questions. Show your workings (on separate paper if necessary) and include the correct units in your answers.

1 **a) Complete the table of values for the graph of $y = x^2 + 4$** (2 marks)

x	-2	-1	0	1	2	3
$y = x^2 + 4$		5				13

b) On the grid, draw the graph of $y = x^2 + 4$ (2 marks)

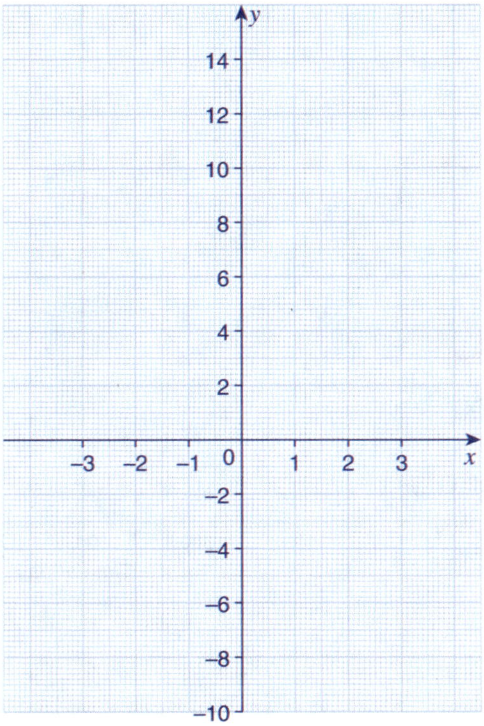

c) Use your graph to find an estimate of:

i) the solutions of the equation $x^2 + 4 = 10$ (1 mark)

$x =$ ....

ii) the solutions of the equation $x^2 + 4 = 13$ (2 marks)

$x =$ ....

Score /7

How well did you do? ✗ 1–4 Try again 5–9 Getting there 10–14 Good work 15–21 Excellent! ✓

For more information on this topic see pages 42–43 of your Success Guide.

Interpreting graphs

A Choose just one answer, a, b, c or d.

1 If £1 = $1.48, how much would £10 be in American dollars? (1 mark)

a) $0.148 b) $148 c) $14.80 d) $1480

For the next three questions use the graph opposite. The graph shows Mrs Morgan's car journey.

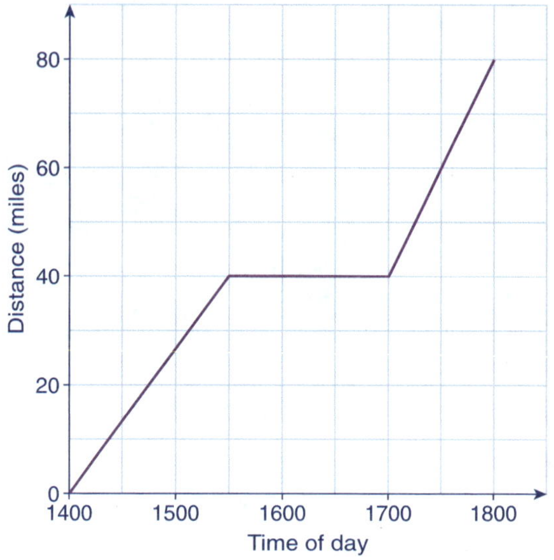

2 At what speed did Mrs Morgan travel for the first hour and a half? (1 mark)

a) 25 mph b) 28 mph
c) 30 mph d) 26.7 mph

3 At what time did Mrs Morgan take a break from her car journey? (1 mark)

a) 1530 b) 1600 c) 1400 d) 1500

4 At what speed did Mrs Morgan travel between 1700 and 1800 hours? (1 mark)

a) 60 mph b) 80 mph
c) 35 mph d) 40 mph

Score / 4

B Answer all parts of the questions.

1 Water is poured into these odd-shaped vases at a constant rate. (3 marks)

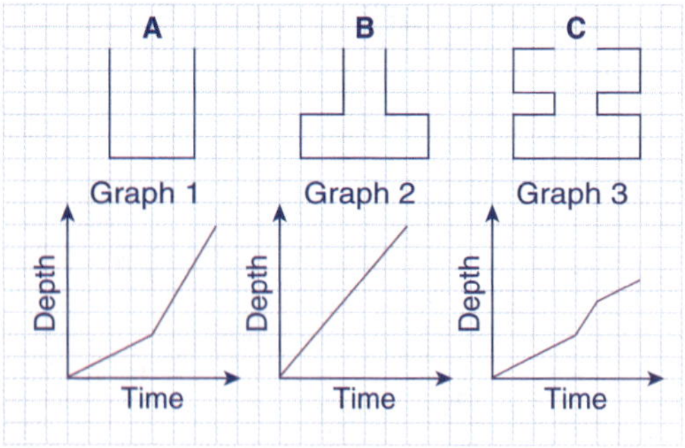

Match each vase to the correct graph.

Vase A matches graph ....

Vase B matches graph ....

Vase C matches graph ....

2 Match these graphs to the statements. (3 marks)

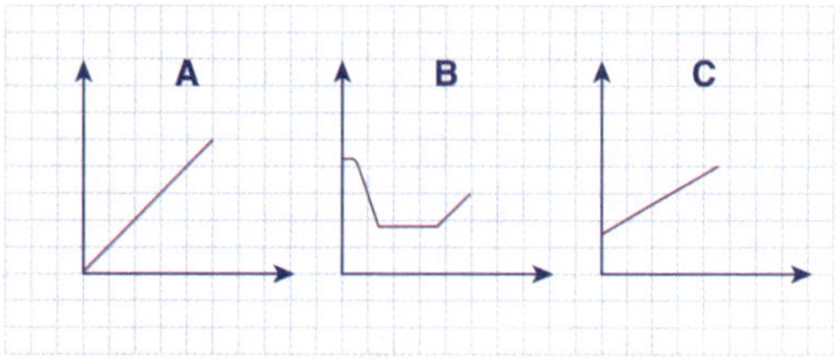

1. A mobile phone company charges a standard fee plus a certain amount per call. Graph ....
2. The price of shares dropped sharply, levelled off and then started rising. Graph ....
3. Conversion between kilometres and miles. Graph ....

Score / 6

C This is a GCSE-style question. Answer all parts of the question. Show your workings (on separate paper if necessary) and include the correct units in your answers.

1 William went for a cycle ride to the local market.
The distance–time graph shows his ride.

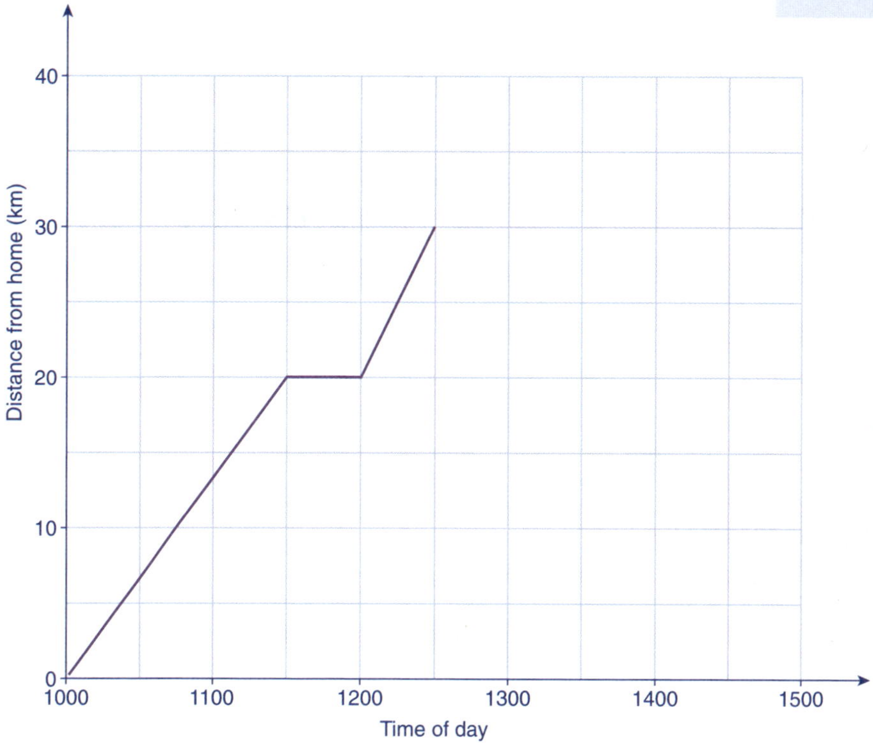

He set off from home at 1000 and arrived at the market at 1230.

a) Explain what might have happened to William when he was 20 kilometres from home. (1 mark)

....

....

b) At what speed did William travel in the first 20 kilometres? (2 marks)

....

William stayed at the market for 30 minutes and then cycled home at 25 kilometres per hour.

c) Complete the distance–time graph to show this information. (3 marks)

d) At approximately what time did William arrive home? .... (1 mark)

Score /7

How well did you do? 1–4 Try again 5–8 Getting there 9–13 Good work 14–17 Excellent!

For more information on this topic see pages 44–45 of your Success Guide.

Shapes

A Choose just one answer, a, b, c or d.

Questions 1–5 relate to the diagrams below.

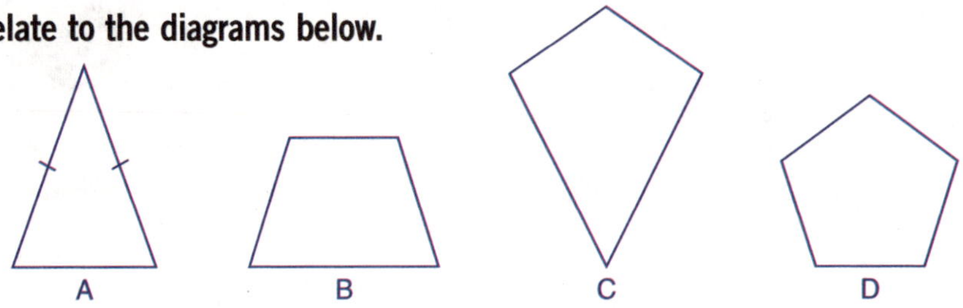

1 What is the name of shape B? (1 mark)

a) triangle b) kite
c) hexagon d) trapezium

2 What is the name of shape D? (1 mark)

a) triangle b) parallelogram
c) hexagon d) pentagon

3 What special type of triangle is shape A? (1 mark)

a) Equilateral b) Scalene
c) Isosceles d) Isolateral

4 How many lines of symmetry does shape C have? (1 mark)

a) 1 b) 2
c) 3 d) 4

5 What is the name of shape C? (1 mark)

a) parallelogram b) kite
c) trapezium d) rectangle

Score / 5

B Answer all parts of the questions.

1 These shapes are quadrilaterals.

Decide whether each of these statements is true or false.

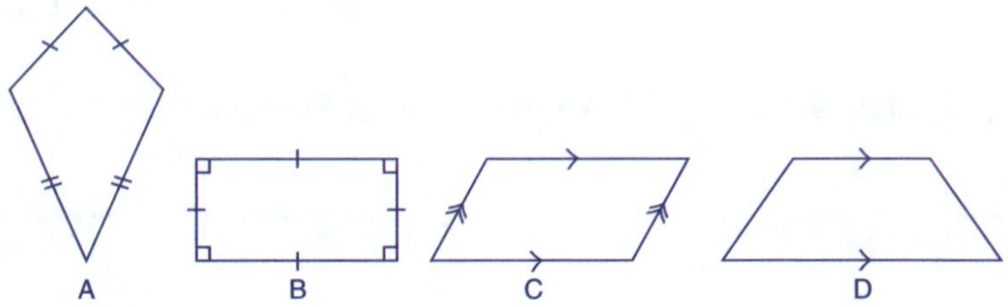

a) Shape B is a rectangle. .... (1 mark)

b) Shape D is a parallelogram .... (1 mark)

c) Shape A has 2 lines of symmetry. .... (1 mark)

d) Shape B has rotational symmetry of order 4. .... (1 mark)

e) Shape C is a parallelogram. .... (1 mark)

2 a) How many lines of symmetry does a regular octagon have? .... (1 mark)

b) What is the order of rotational symmetry of a regular hexagon? .... (1 mark)

3 Draw an equilateral triangle in the space below. (2 marks)

Score / 9

SHAPES

Shape, Space and Measures

C

These are GCSE-style questions. Answer all parts of the questions. Show your workings (on separate paper if necessary) and include the correct units in your answers.

1 **Some names of polygons have been written on cards.**

Hexagon	**Pentagon**	**Octagon**	**Triangle**	**Quadrilateral**

Write down the name of the polygon for each of the shapes below, choosing from the above cards. (4 marks)

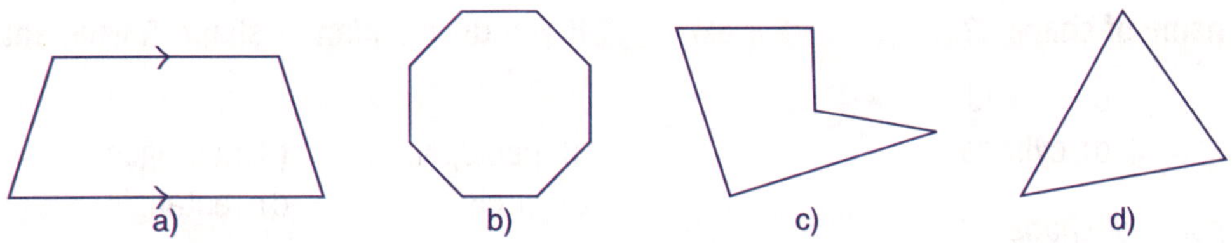

a) .... b) ....

c) .... d) ....

2 **In the space provided, draw an example of each of these shapes.** (4 marks)

a) Parallelogram

b) Hexagon

c) Trapezium

d) Rhombus

3 **The diagram shows parts of a circle.**
Choose the correct label for each part of the circle. (4 marks)

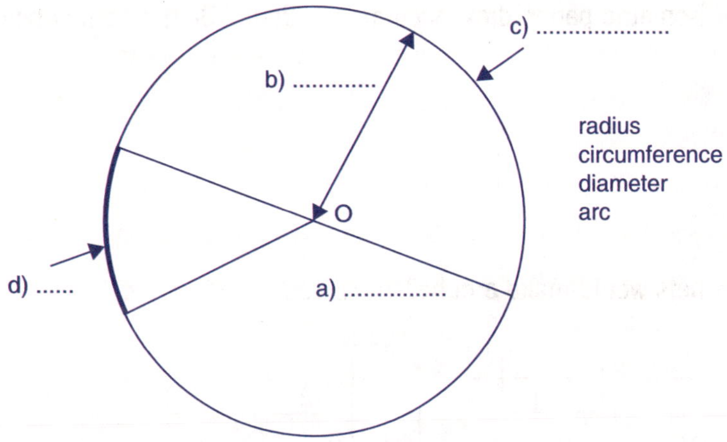

Score / 12

How well did you do? 1–7 Try again 8–11 Getting there 12–17 Good work 18–26 Excellent!

For more information on this topic see pages 48–49 of your Success Guide.

Solids

A Choose just one answer, a, b, c or d.

Questions 1–5 relate to the diagrams below.

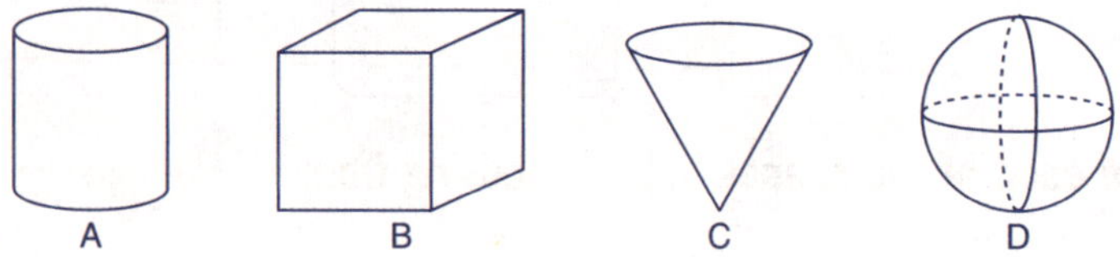

1 What is the name of shape C? (1 mark)

a) cube b) cuboid
c) cone d) cylinder

2 What is the name of shape D? (1 mark)

a) cube b) sphere
c) cuboid d) cone

3 What is the name of shape A? (1 mark)

a) rhombus b) cone
c) cylinder d) sphere

4 If you draw a plan of shape A what shape will it be? (1 mark)

a) pentagon b) heptagon
c) circle d) rectangle

5 How many edges does shape B have? (1 mark)

a) 12 b) 8
c) 9 d) 10

Score / 5

B Answer all parts of the questions.

1 In the spaces below write down the correct mathematical name of each object. (3 marks)

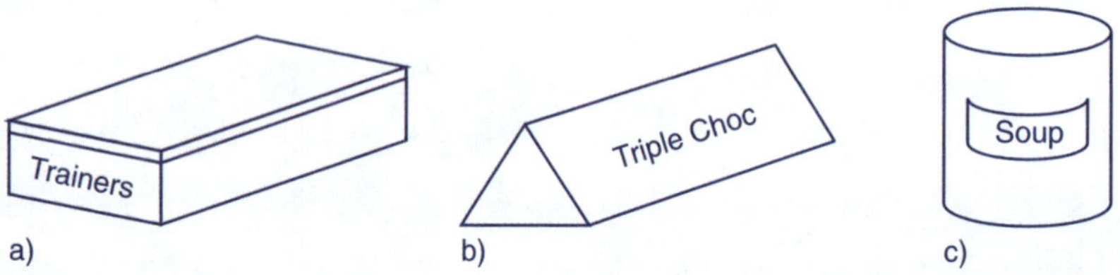

a) .... b) .... c) ....

2 On a separate piece of isometric paper, draw accurately a 2cm x 3cm x 4cm cuboid. (3 marks)

3 Which of the following nets would make a cube? .... (1 mark)

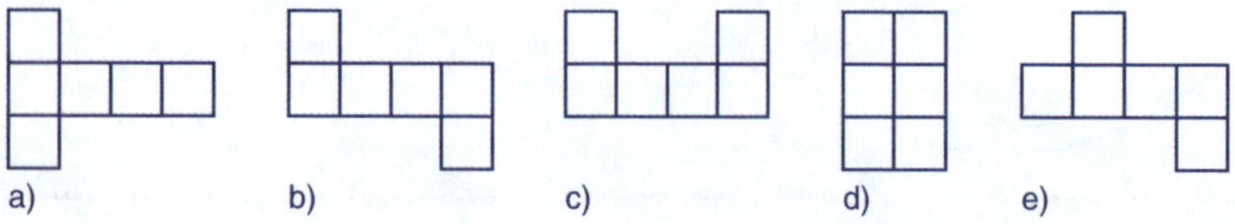

Score / 7

Letts and LONSDALE

endorsed by edexcel

GCSE Success

Workbook Answer Booklet

Edexcel Mathematics Foundation

for the linear and modular specifications

GCSE Mathematics Foundation Edexcel

Answer Booklet

Answers

NUMBER

Page 6 – Number revision

A

1. d
2. c
3. a
4. c
5. d

B

1. a) six hundred and two
   b) five thousand seven hundred and twenty nine
2. a) 436
   b) 6 000 405
3. a) 3 tens
   b) 3 thousands
   c) 3 hundred thousands
4. a) 6, 47, 75, 93, 102, 827, 1436
   b) 159, 729, 3692, 4138, 4207, 4879

C

1. a) 1700
   b) 170 000
2. a) 16 431
   b) 3 ten thousands = 30 000
   c) 2358
3. a) 10
   b) 3, 6, 9, 12, 15, 18
4. a) 18, 61, 72, 104, 130
   b) 18, 19, 62, 397, 407

Page 8 – Numbers

A

1. d
2. b
3. b
4. c
5. a

B

1. a) true b) false
   c) false d) false
2. a) ±2 b) ±10
   c) 64 d) 2
   e) −5 f) 225
3. $72 = 2^3 \times 3^2$
4. $a = 2$, $b = 2$
5. 60
6. 8
7. true

C

1. a) 1, 9, 16, 25
   b) 1, 6, 12, 24
   c) 11, 17
   d) 9
2. Since $\sqrt{64} = 8$, then $\sqrt{60}$ must be less than 8
3. a) i) $56 = 2 \times 2 \times 2 \times 7$
   ii) $60 = 2 \times 2 \times 3 \times 5$
   b) HCF = 4
   c) LCM = 840
4. $360 = 2^3 \times 3^2 \times 5$
   Hence $a = 3$, $b = 2$, $c = 1$

Page 10 – Positive and negative numbers

A

1. b
2. c
3. a
4. d
5. b

B

1. a) −7 and 5
   b) −7 and −3
   c) 5 and −7
2. −3 × 4 — −12
   12 ÷ (−2) — −6
   −4 − (−3) — −1
   −5 × (−2) — 10
   −20 ÷ (−5) — 4
3. a) 10
   b) −10
   c) 14
4.

	-16		
	-5	-11	
3	-8	-3	
5	-2	-6	3

C

1. a) 18°C
   b) i) 17°C
   ii) 19°C
2. a) 12°C
   b) 4°C
   c) −11°C

Page 12 – Working with numbers

A

1. b
2. c
3. a
4. b
5. d

B

1. 6 × 10 — 60
   70 × 1000 — 70 000
   240 ÷ 100 — 2.4
   600 ÷ 1000 — 0.6
   80 × 30 — 2400
2. a) 421 b) 365
   c) 15 888 d) 832
3. a) 7254 b) 7632
   c) 17 d) 48
4. £8804

C

1. a)

Item	Cost	Number bought	Total Cost
Bread	79p	4	£3.16
Milk	72p	2	£1.44
Cleaning fluid	£2.76	2	£5.52

   b) £5.12
2. a) 2976 sheets of paper
   b) 6 reams of paper
3. a) £5.15
   b) 12 packs of squared paper.
4. a) 13 392
   b) 47

Page 14 – Fractions

A

1. c
2. a
3. b
4. c
5. a

B

1. a) $\frac{4}{22}$ b) $\frac{28}{49}$
   c) $\frac{1}{4}$ d) $\frac{36}{51}$
2. a) $2\frac{1}{2}$ b) $1\frac{2}{3}$
   c) $4\frac{1}{2}$ d) $1\frac{1}{11}$
3. a) $\frac{5}{9}$ b) $\frac{17}{44}$
   c) $\frac{3}{14}$ d) 3
   e) $\frac{2}{3}$ f) $\frac{5}{9}$
   g) $\frac{7}{8}$ h) $\frac{11}{12}$
4. a) $\frac{1}{7}$ $\frac{3}{10}$ $\frac{1}{2}$ $\frac{2}{3}$ $\frac{3}{4}$ $\frac{4}{5}$
   b) $\frac{1}{9}$ $\frac{2}{7}$ $\frac{1}{3}$ $\frac{2}{5}$ $\frac{5}{8}$ $\frac{3}{4}$
5. a) true b) false

C

1. Jonathan, since $\frac{2}{3}$ is greater than $\frac{3}{5}$.
2. a) $1\frac{7}{15}$ b) $\frac{16}{33}$
   c) $\frac{8}{63}$ d) $\frac{3}{4}$
3. $\frac{7}{15}$
4. 28 students
5. 13 sweets

Page 16 – Decimals

A

1. c
2. c
3. b
4. d
5. b

B

1. a) false b) true
   c) true d) true
   e) true
2. 7.09, 7.102, 7.32, 7.321, 8.31, 8.315
3. a) Molly
   b) 1.201 seconds
   c) 0.002 seconds
4. a) 16 b) 100
   c) 2000 d) 0.1
   e) 24 f) 0.01

C

1. a) 6.14, 6.141, 7.208, 7.29, 7.42
   b) 1.28
   c) 34.199
   d) i) 7.21
   ii) 6.14
2. a) 0.01
   b) 0.1
   c) 0.001
3. a) $\frac{629}{1000}$
   b) 0.28

Page 18 – Percentages 1

A

1. c
2. c
3. a
4. d
5. d

B

1. 10% of 30 — 3
   40% of 40 — 16
   5% of 15 — 0.75
   25% of 20 — 5
2. £26 265
3. £102
4. 77%
5. £1.80
6. 40%

C

1 a) £30.63 b) £339.15
2. £29.90
3. £4307.55

Page 20 – Percentages 2

A

1. d
2. a
3. c
4. b

B

1. £168.03
2. £75.60
3. £6969.60
4. £391.51
5. £135 475.20
6. 121.2p

C

1. a) £1000 b) £160
2. 1.61m
3. a) 3.5% b) £756
4. £11 340

Page 22 – Fractions, decimals and percentages

A

1. c
2. b
3. d
4. d
5. a

B

1.

Fraction	Decimal	Percentage
$\frac{2}{5}$	**0.4**	**40%**
$\frac{1}{20}$	**0.05**	5%
$\frac{1}{3}$	$0.\dot{3}$	**$33.\dot{3}$%**
$\frac{1}{25}$	0.04	**4%**
$\frac{1}{4}$	**0.25**	25%
$\frac{1}{8}$	**0.125**	**12.5%**

2. 30%, $\frac{1}{3}$, 0.37, $\frac{3}{8}$, $\frac{1}{2}$, 0.62, 92%
3. 'Rosebushes' is cheaper because $\frac{1}{4} = 25\%$ which is greater than the reduction at 'Gardens are Us'.

C

1. $\frac{1}{8}$, 25%, 0.27, $\frac{1}{3}$, $\frac{2}{5}$, 0.571, 72%
2. Ed's Electricals: £225
   Sheila's Bargains: £217.38
   Gita's TV shop: £232
   Maximum price = £232
   Minimum price = £217.38
3. Both will give the same answer because increasing by 20% is the same as multiplying by 1.2. Finding 10% then doubling it gives 20%, which when you add it to 40, is the same as increasing £40 by 20%.
4. $\frac{1}{10}$, $\frac{3}{5}$, $\frac{5}{8}$, $\frac{2}{3}$, $\frac{9}{10}$

Page 24 – Approximations and using a calculator

A

1. b
2. d
3. c
4. c
5. d

B

1. a) true b) false
   c) false d) true
2. a) 100
   b) 90
3. a) 365 (3 s.f.)
   b) 10.2 (3 s.f.)
   c) 6 320 (3 s.f.)
4. 6×10^9
5. True

C

1. a) 30 and 80
   b) 2 400
   c) 49
2. 7.09 (3 s.f.)
3. a) 5.9371025
   b) $\frac{30 \times 6}{40 - 10} = \frac{180}{30} = 6$
4. $\frac{5}{2}$
5. a) −856.85965
   b) −857

Page 26 – Ratio

A

1. c
2. d
3. c
4. d
5. b

B

1. a) 1 : 1.5
   b) $1 : 1.\dot{6}$
   c) 1 : 3
2. 1200 ml
3. a) £10.25
   b) 48 g
4. £25 000
5. 4.5 days

C

1. £10.14
2. Vicky £6400
   Tracy £8000
3. butter 125 g
   sugar 100 g
   eggs 5
   flour 112.5 g
   milk 37.5 ml
4. 6 days
5. The litre bottle gives the better value for money: 25 cl × 4 = 1 litre, to the cost of the four 0.5 cl bottles would be £2.44, while the 1 litre bottle costs £1.52.

Page 28 – Indices

A

1. a
2. b
3. d
4. d
5. a

B

1. a) 64
   b) 32
   c) 81
2. a) false
   b) false
   c) true
   d) true
   e) false
   f) true
3. a) $6a^2$
   b) $3m^2$
   c) $20a^3b^5$
   d) n^{16}
   e) a^6
   f) $\frac{3}{4a^3}$
   g) $12a^{11}$
   h) $3b^2$
4. a) $n = 6$
   b) $n = 10$
   c) $n = 1$

C

1. a) i) 16
   ii) 27
   b) 9^5
2. a) p^7 b) n^4
   c) a^6 d) $4ab$
3. a) 3
   b) 25
   c) 648
4. a) i) 8
   ii) 36
   iii) 32
   b) 5^4
5. a) $6a^5$
   b) $3a$
   c) $\frac{1}{4b^2}$
6. a) i) 49
   ii) 243
   iii) 16
   b) 3^8

ALGEBRA

Page 30 – Algebra 1

A

1. b
2. c
3. d
4. d
5. c

B

1. a) true
   b) true
   c) false
2. $T = 6b + 0.67m$
3. a) 4
   b) 1.25
   c) 8

C

1. × 4 − 2

Input	Output
1	2
2	6
4	14
6	22
9	34

2. a) $2t$
   b) $3y^2$
3. a) $6n$
   b) $6ab$
4. a) $p = 5n - 6$
   b) $p = -16$
5. 2.64
6. She has forgotten to take the square root of 37 to find v.

Page 32 – Algebra 2

A

1. a
2. c
3. d
4. c
5. a

B

1. a) $3n - 9$ b) $5(n + 3)$
   c) $n^2 - 3n + 2$ d) $8(n + 2)$
2. a) $5(2n + 3)$
   b) $12(2 - 3n)$
   c) $5(1 + 2n)$
   d) $4(5 - n)$
   e) $6a(a + 2)$
3. a) $b = \frac{p + 4}{3}$
   b) $b = \frac{4y + 6}{a}$
   c) $b = \frac{2 - 5n}{3}$
4. True

C

1. a) $4x + 4$
   b) i) $6(a + 2)$
   ii) $5a(2a - 3b)$
2. a) $x = \frac{p + 2y}{5}$
   b) $x = 2p + 2$
3. $n(n + 2) - 3(n - 1)$
   $= n^2 + 2n - 3n + 3$
   $= n^2 - n + 3$
4. a) $5a$
   b) i) $3(n - 4)$
   ii) $4p(2q - 3)$
5. a) $a = b + 5h$
   $a - b = 5h$
   $h = \frac{a - b}{5}$
   b) $a = b + 5h$
   $a = 4 + 5 \times -2$
   $= 4 - 10$
   $a = -6$
   c) i) $3(n + 4) + 2(n - 1)$
   $= 3n + 12 + 2n - 2$
   $= 5n + 10 = 5(n + 2)$
   ii) $5(2n - 1) - 3(n + 2)$
   $= 10n - 5 - 3n - 6$
   $= 7n - 11$

Page 34 – Equations 1

A

1. c
2. a
3. d
4. b
5. c

B

1. a) $n = 9$
   b) $n = 2$
   c) $n = 2$
   d) $n = -7$
   e) $n = 18$
   f) $n = 1$
2. 1
3. a) $n = 5$
   b) $n = 3$
   c) $n = 7$
   d) $n = -5.5$
   e) $n = 25$
   f) $n = 4$
4. a) $n = 3$
   b) $n = 5$
   c) $n = 4$
   d) $n = 14$

C

1. a) $n = 4$
   b) $n = 3$
   c) $n = 5$
   d) $n = 14$
2. a) $m = 3$
   b) $p = \frac{6}{10}$ or $p = \frac{3}{5}$
   c) $x = 6$
   d) $x = 6$
3. a) $x = 16$
   b) $x = 10$
   c) $x = 7$
   d) $x = -3$
4. a) 6 b) $x = 1$

Page 36 – Equations 2 and inequalities

A

1. c
2. c
3. c
4. d
5. c

B

1. 5.6, −3.6
2. a) $x < 2$
   b) $x \geq 6$
   c) $1 \leq x \leq 4$
   d) $\frac{1}{3} \leq x \leq 2$
3. $2n + (n + 30°) + (n - 10°) = 180$
   $4n + 20° = 180°$
   $n = 40°$

C

1. a) −3, −2, −1, 0, 1, 2
   b) $p \leq 2$
2. $x = 2.7$
3. a) $9x + 4$
   b) $x = 2$; shortest side = 3 cm
4. $x = 2.8$

Page 38 – Number patterns and sequences

A

1. d
2. a
3. c
4. b

B

1. a) 10, 12 b) 16, 19
   c) 47, 57 d) 0.75, 0.375
2. a) even numbers
   b) powers of 10
   c) cube numbers
3. a) 22
   b) $3n + 4$
4. a) false
   b) false
   c) true
5. 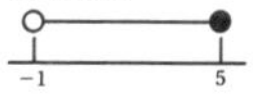

6. $x < 4$

C

1. a) 

   b)

Pattern number	1	2	3	4	5	6
Number of dots	10	14	18	22	26	30

   c) 54
2. a) 13, 15
   b) add 2 to the preceeding term.
3. a) 2, 1, $\frac{1}{2}$
   b) $5n - 3$
4. $4n - 1$
5. 2, 3

Page 40 – Straight-line graphs

A

1. b
2. d
3. b
4. c
5. a

B

1. a)

x	−2	−1	0	1	2
y	**8**	**7**	6	**5**	4

b) i)

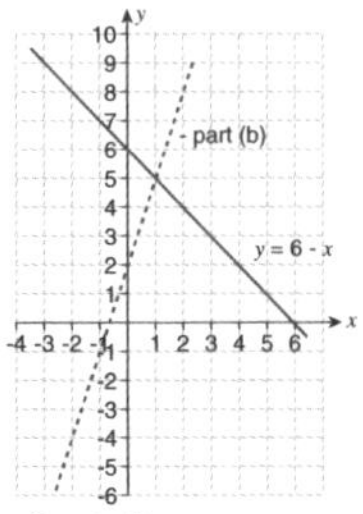

ii) $y = 3x + 2$

c) (1, 5)

2. $y = 3 - 2x$ and $y = 4 - 2x$

C

1. a) Gradient = −1

b)

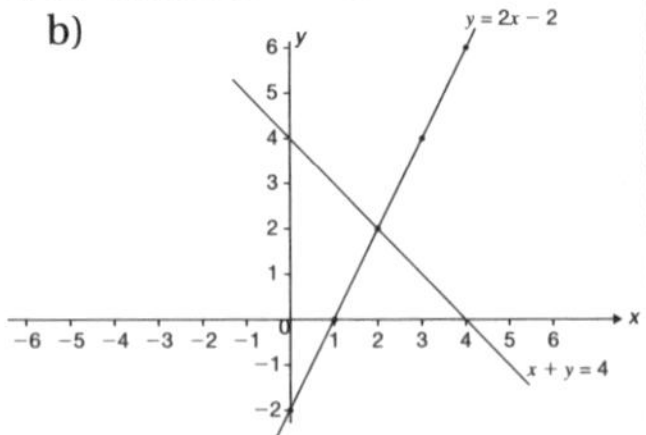

c) (2, 2)

d) $x = 2\frac{1}{2}$

2. a) $y = 2x \pm k$, where k is any number

b) No, they are not parallel because the gradients are not the same. The gradient of $y = 3x - 2$ is 3, of $y = 4x + 1$ is 4.

Page 42 – Curved graphs

A

1. b
2. d
3. c
4. d
5. b

B

1. a)

x	−2	−1	0	1	2	3
y	**6**	**1**	−2	**−3**	**−2**	1

b)

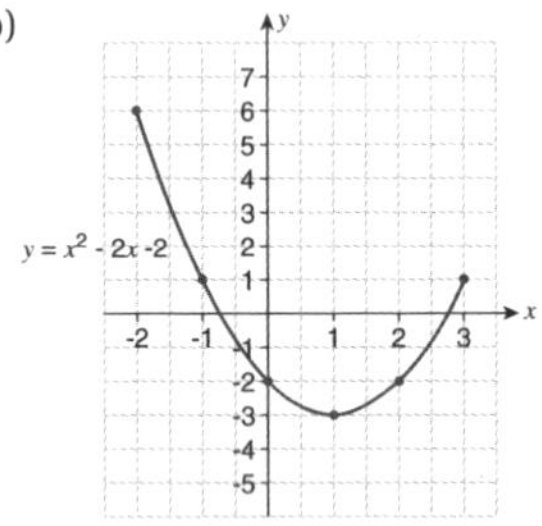

c) i) $x = 0, x = 2$

ii) $x = 2.73$ or -0.73

C

1. a)

x	−2	−1	0	1	2	3
y	**8**	5	**4**	**5**	**8**	13

b)

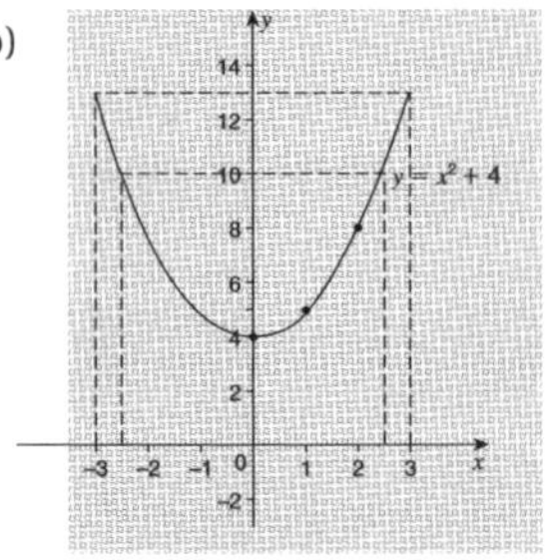

c) i) $x = \pm2.4$ ii) $x = \pm3$

Page 44 – Interpreting graphs

A

1. c
2. d
3. a
4. d

B

1. Vase A matches graph 2
   Vase B matches graph 1
   Vase C matches graph 3
2. Statement 1 with graph C
   Statement 2 with graph B
   Statement 3 with graph A

C

1. a) He may have decided to have a rest, met somebody and stopped to talk, had a flat tyre.
   (Any reasonable explanation, which implies that he stopped.)

   b) 13.$\dot{3}$ km/h

   c)

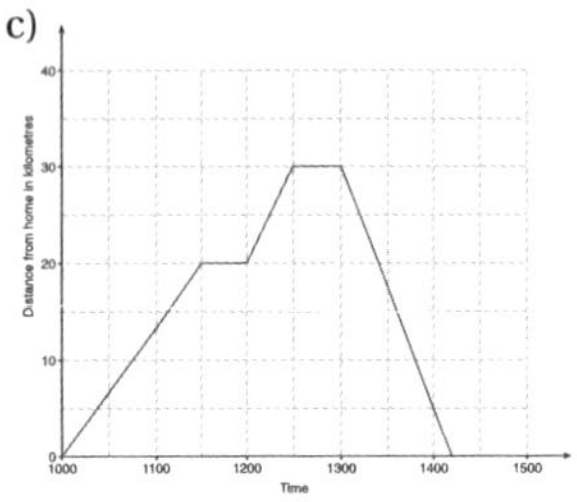

   d) approximately 1415

SHAPE, SPACE AND MEASURES

Page 46 – Shapes

A

1. d
2. d
3. c
4. a
5. b

B

1. a) true
   b) false
   c) false
   d) false
   e) true
2. a) eight
   b) six
3. (A triangle with three equal sides and three angles of 60° should be drawn).

C

1. a) Quadrilateral
   b) Octagon
   c) Pentagon
   d) Triangle
2.

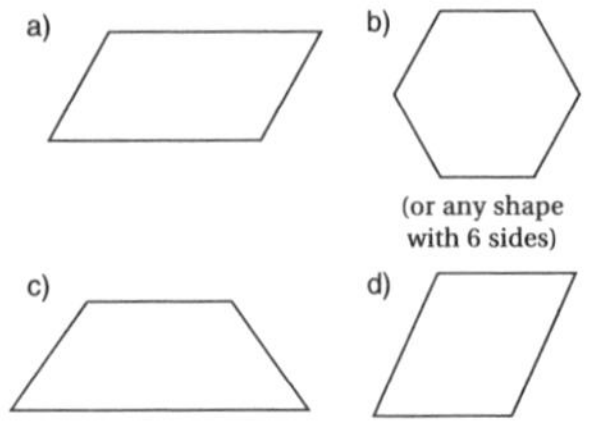

3.

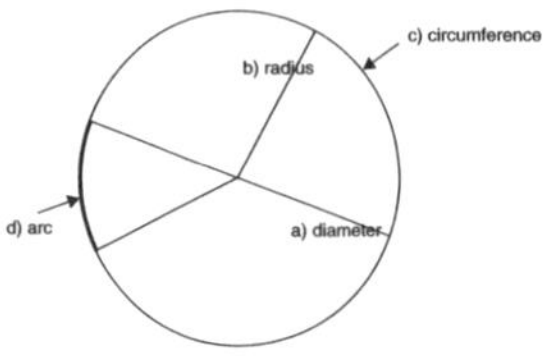

Page 48 – Solids

A

1. c
2. b
3. c
4. c
5. a

B

1. a) Cuboid
   b) Triangular prism
   c) Cylinder
2.

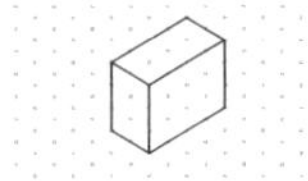

3. a, b and e

C

1. a) Triangular prism
   b) Cylinder
2.

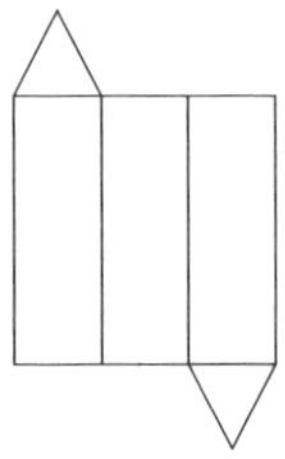

3.

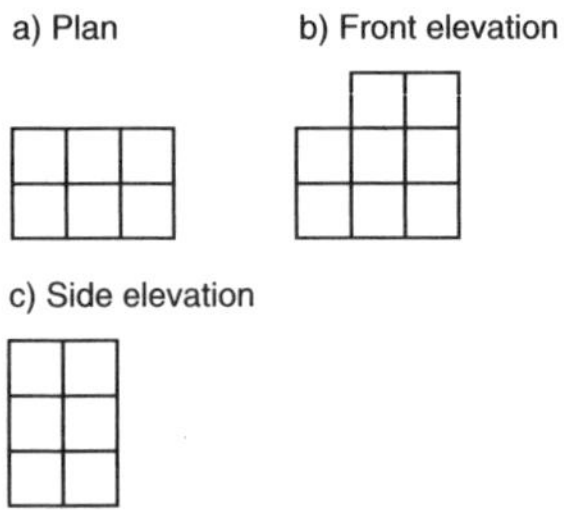

Page 50 – Symmetry and constructions

A

1. a
2. d
3. a
4. c
5. b

B

1. a) **Accept any other planes of symmetry**

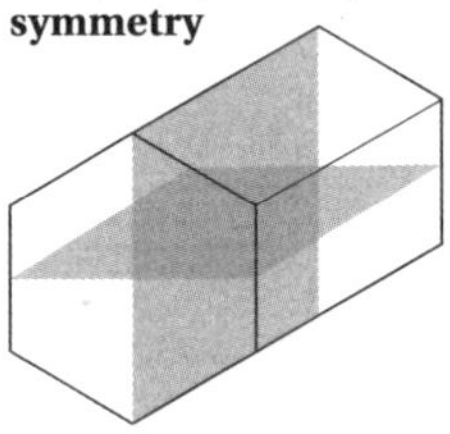

b)

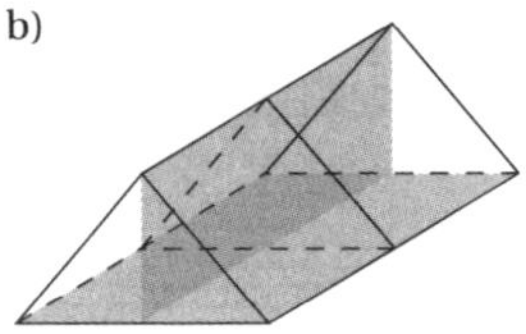

2. a)

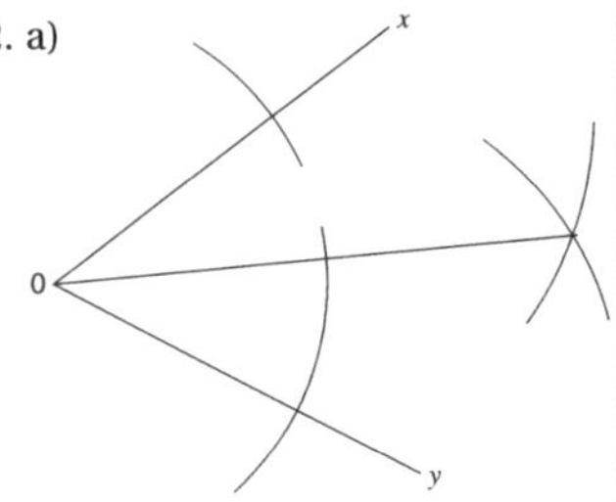

b) 50°

3.

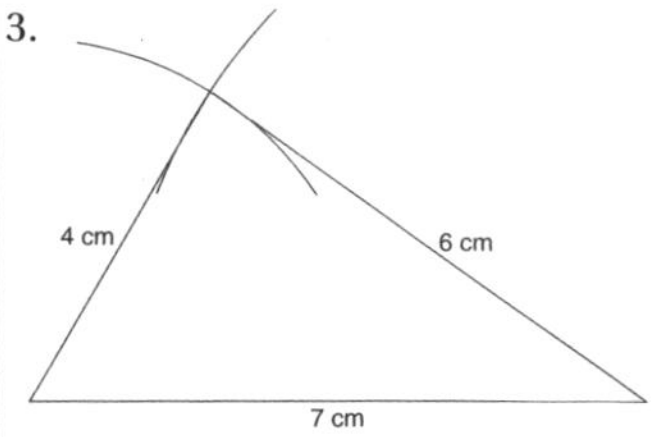

C

1. a)

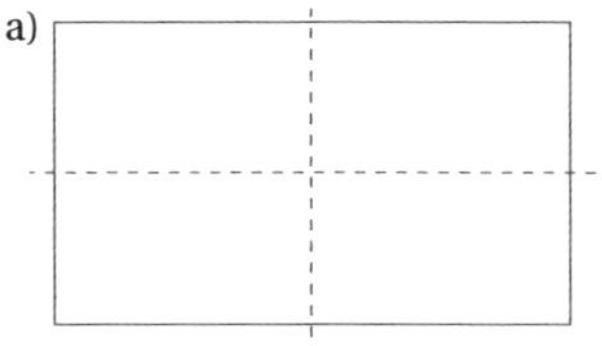

b) order 2

2.

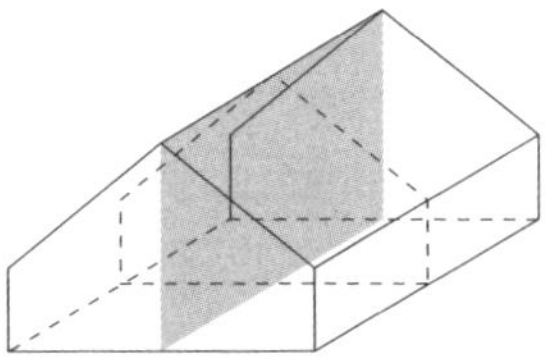

3.

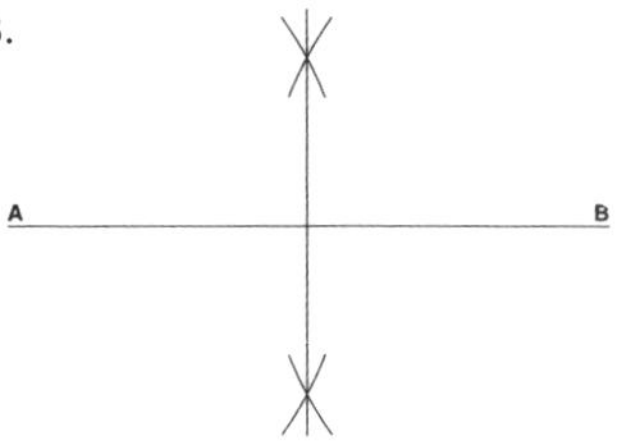

Page 52 – Angles

A

1. a
2. c
3. b
4. b
5. a

B

1. a) $n = 65°$ b) $n = 63°$
   c) $n = 148°$ d) $n = 68°$
   e) $n = 91°$ f) $n = 60°$
   g) $n = 154°$
2.

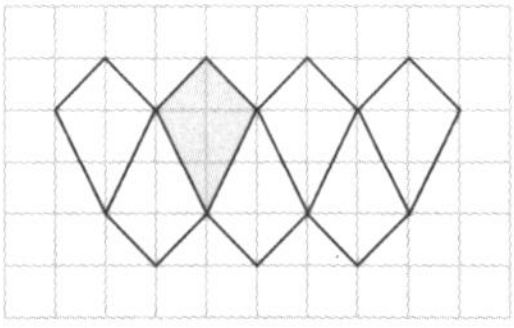

C

1. a) i) $x = 18°$
   ii) If AB is vertical and BD is horizontal, ABE = 90°. So angle x must be 18°.
   b) i) $y = 54°$
   ii) Triangle BCD is isosceles, so angles BDC and BCD are equal. Hence y must be 54°.
   c) i) $z = 54°$
   ii) Angle z is an alternate angle with angle BDC since CF and BE are parallel.
2. Sum of interior angles in a hexagon = $(2n - 4) \times 90°$. Sum of angles in a hexagon is 720°. Angle $x = 105°$

Page 54 – Bearings and scale drawings

A

1. c
2. a
3. d
4. b

B

1. 10 km
2. a)

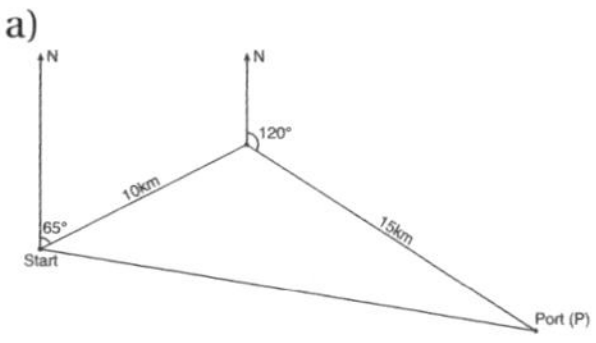

b) 11.1 cm = 22.2 km

c) 099°

3. false, it is 240°

C

1. a) i) 325 m
   ii) 060°
   iii) 120°
   b)

2. Lengths of 4.5 cm, 6 cm and 7 cm must be ± 2 mm.

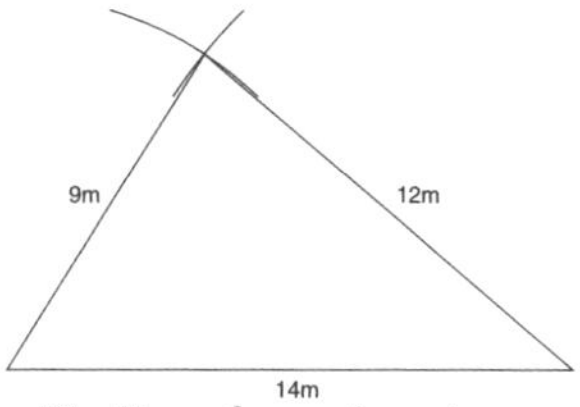

Page 56 – Transformations 1

A

1. a
2. c
3. b
4. b

B

1.

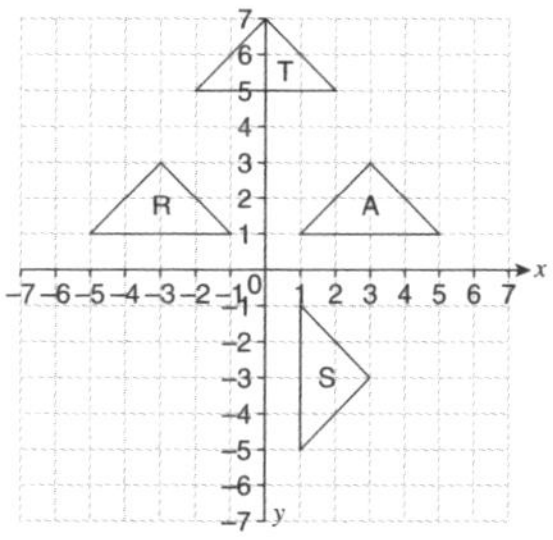

2. a) translation
   b) rotation
   c) translation
   d) reflection

C

1. a) reflection in the x axis
   b) rotation 90° anticlockwise about (0, 0)
2.

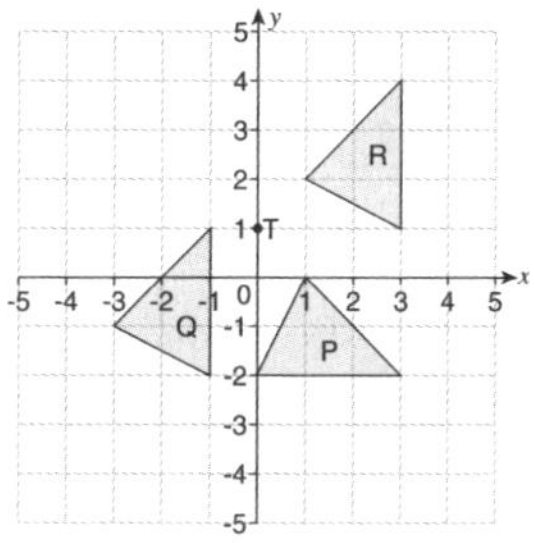

Page 58 – Transformations 2

A

1. d
2. b
3. b

B

1.

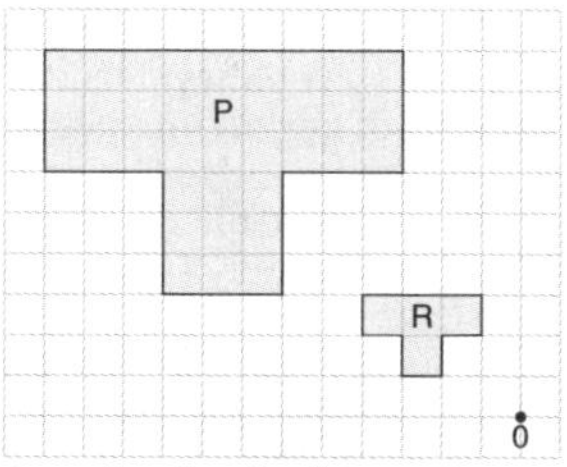

2. a) reflection in the y axis
   b) rotation 90° clockwise about (0, 0)
   c) reflection in the line y = x

C

1. a)

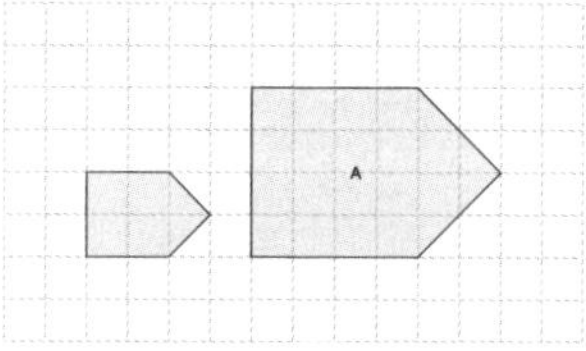

b) 20 cm^2

2.

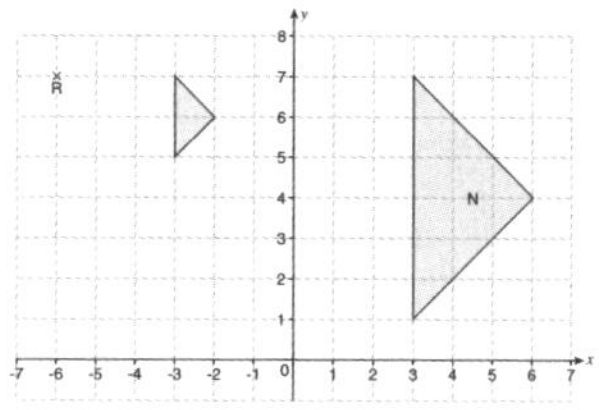

Page 60 – Loci and coordinates

A

1. c
2. d
3. a
4. d
5. b

B

1.

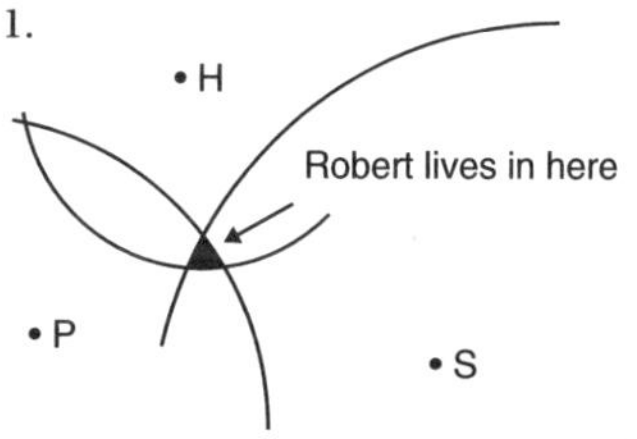

2. R = (3, 0, 3)
   S = (3, 3, 1)
   T = (0, 3, 1)
   U = (0, 1, 1)

C

1.

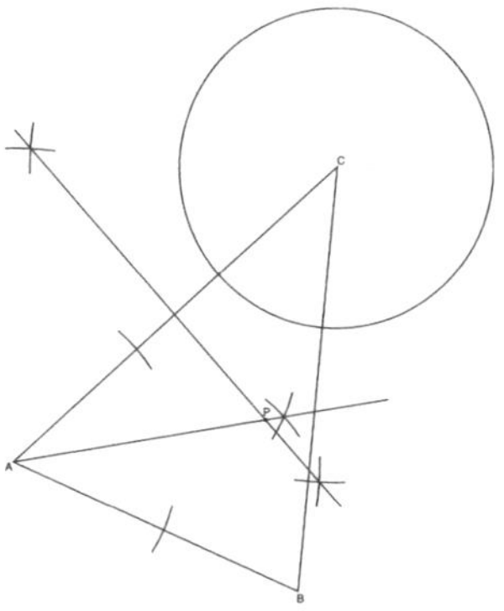

2. (5,4,0)

Page 62 – Pythagoras' theorem

A

1. d
2. b
3. a
4. c

B

1. a) n = 15 cm
   b) n = 12.6 cm
   c) n = 15.1 cm
   d) n = 24. 6 cm
2. Since
   $12^2 + 5^2 = 13^2$
   $144 + 25 = 169$
   the triangle must be right-angled for Pythagoras' Theorem to be applied.
3. Both statements are true:
   Length of line = $\sqrt{(6^2 + 3^2)}$
   = $\sqrt{45}$ = 6.7 (1dp)
   Midpoint = $\left(\frac{2+5}{2}\right), \left(\frac{11+5}{2}\right)$
   = (3.5, 8)

C

1. 7.8 cm
2. 24.1 cm
3. 13.7 cm
4. 6.4 cm

Page 64 – Measures and measurement 1

A

1. b
2. a
3. d
4. d
5. a

B

1.

12-hour clock	24-hour clock
4:23 pm	**1623**
3:34 pm	1534
9:26 pm	2126
3:16 pm	**1516**
3:14 am	0314
9:38 pm	**2138**

2. a) 10–15 m
   b) about 240 km
   c) 5 ml
3.

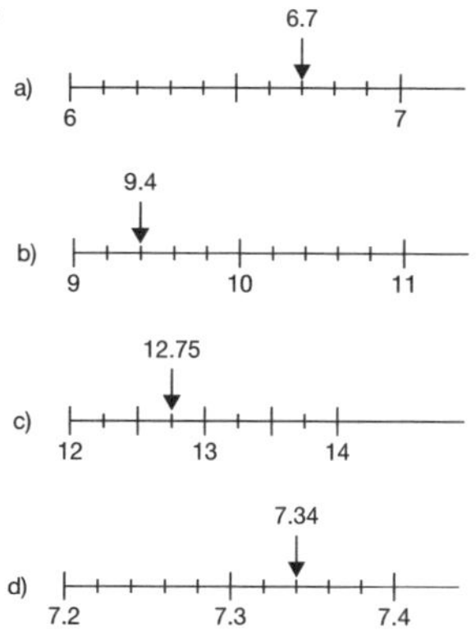

C

1. a) 19.6
   b) 20
   c)

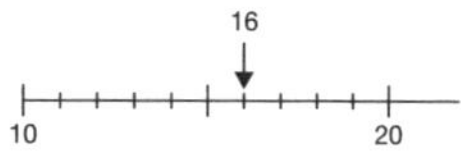

d)

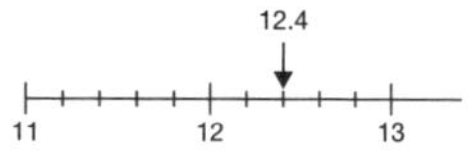

2. a) 20 minutes
   b) 50 minutes
   c) 22 minutes
   d) 51 minutes

Page 66 – Measures and measurement 2

A

1. b
2. d
3. a
4. d
5. c

B

1. a) 8000 m
   b) 3.25 kg
   c) 7000 kg
   d) 0.52 m
   e) 2700 ml
   f) 0.00262 km
2. 12.5 miles
3. 1.32 pounds
4. Lower limit = 46.5 m
   Upper limit = 47.5 m
5. $53.\dot{3}$ mph
6. 0.1 g/cm^3

C

1. a) 17.6 pounds
   b) 48 kilometres
2. 80 kg
3. a) 1 hour 36 minutes
   b) Average speed $4.\dot{4}$ km/h
4. Length = 12.05 cm
   Width = 5.5 cm
5. a) 111.5g
   a) 112.5g

Page 68 – Area of 2D shapes

A

1. c
2. d
3. b
4. d
5. b

B

1. a) false
   b) true
   c) true
   d) false
2. 38.6 cm
3. 84.21 cm^2

C

1. 81 cm^2
2. 38.8 cm
3. 127 cm (to nearest cm)
4. 120.24 cm^2

Page 70 – Volume of 3D shapes

A

1. a
2. c
3. a
4. c
5. d

B

1. Emily is not correct.
   The correct volume is 345.6 ÷ 2 172.8 m^3
2. Volume = 170.2 m^3
3. Height = 9.9 cm
4. Volume needs three dimensions.
   $V = 4r^2$ is only two-dimensional, hence this must be a formula for area, not volume.

MATHS SUCCESS Answers

C

1. 64 cm^3
2. a) 672 cm^3
   b) 0.000672 m^3
3. a) 288 cm^2
   b) 240 cm^3
4. $4r^2p$ volume
   $3\pi\sqrt{r^2 + p^2}$ length
   $\frac{4\pi r^2}{3p}$ length
5. 3807 cm^3

HANDLING DATA

Page 72 – Collecting data

A

1. b
2. d
3. a
4. b

B

1.

type of book	tally	frequency

2. The tick boxes overlap. Which box would somebody who did 2 hours of homework tick? It needs an extra box for 5 or more hours.
   How much time do you spend to the nearest hour, doing homework each night?
   0 up to 1 hour
   1 up to 2 hours
   2 up to 3 hours
   3 up to 4 hours
   4 up to 5 hours
   5 hours and over
3. She is asking only men and not both men and women. She is also asking men who are interested in football as they are going to a football match, so her results will be biased.

C

1

Colour of vehicles	Tally	Frequency

2. From the list below tick your favourite chocolate bar.
   Mars ☐ Twix ☐
   Toblerone ☐ Galaxy ☐
   Bounty ☐ Snickers ☐
   Other ....
3. The key to this question is to break the question into subgroups.
   1 On average how many hours **per day** do you watch television?
   0 up to 1 hour ☐
   1 up to 2 hours ☐
   2 up to 3 hours ☐
   3 up to 4 hours ☐
   Over 4 hours ☐
   2 On average, how many hours **at the weekend** do you watch television?
   0 up to 2 hours ☐
   2 up to 4 hours ☐
   4 up to 6 hours ☐
   6 up to 8 hours ☐
   Over 8 hours ☐

Page 74 – Representing data

A

1. d
2. c
3. a
4. b

B

1.

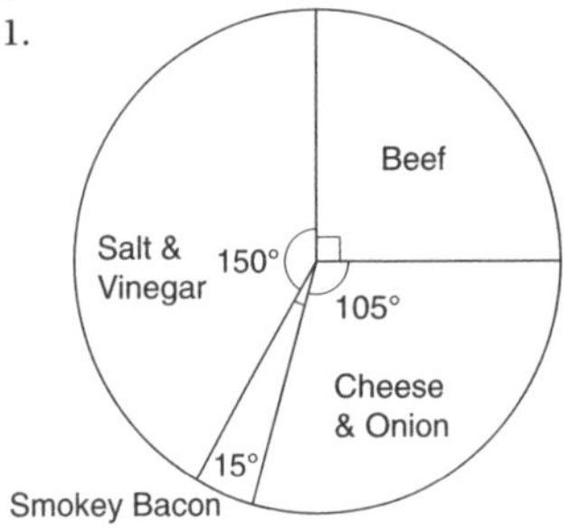

2.

Day	1	2	3	4	5	6	7
Hours of sunshine	3	**4**	1.5	1	1	3	**1.5**

C

1. a) i) 14
   ii) 17
   b) Sunday 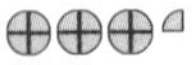
   Monday 
2. a) 390
   b) 390 + (150 × 10p) + (270 × 50p) + (90 × 20p) + (180 × 5p)
   Total £567.
3.

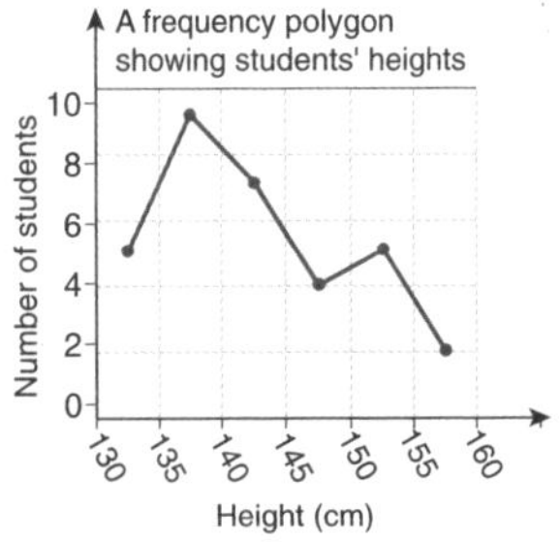

Page 76 – Scatter diagrams and correlation

A

1. c
2. a
3. b

B

1. a) Positive correlation
   b) Negative correlation
   c) Positive correlation
   d) No correlation
2. a) Positive correlation
   b)

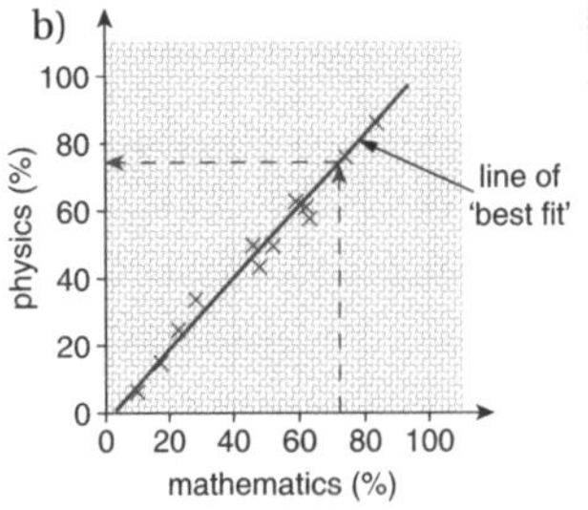

   c) Approximately 74%

C

1. a)

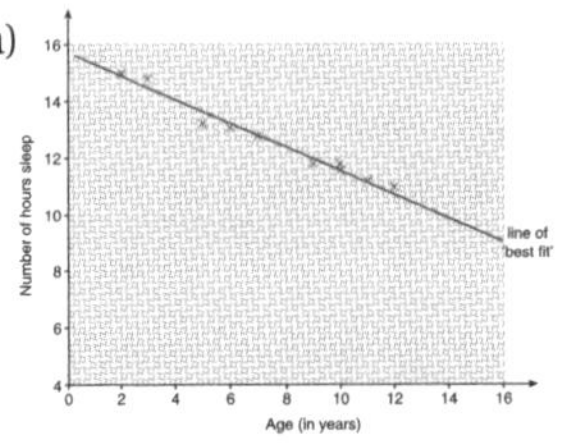

   b) Negative correlation – the younger the child, the more hours sleep they needed.
   c) Line of best fit on diagram above
   d) A four-year-old child needs approximately 14 hours' sleep.
   e) This only gives an estimate as it follows the trend of the data. Similarly, if you continued the line it would suggest that you may eventually need no hours sleep at a certain age, which is not the case.

Page 78 – Averages 1

A

1. c
2. b
3. d
4. d
5. b

B

1. a) false
   b) true
   c) false
   d) true
2. a) mean = 141.35
   b) The manufacturer is justified in making this claim since the mean is nearly 141 and the mode and median are also 141.
3. $x = 17$

C

1. a) 11.5
   b) 8
   c) 10.6 (1 d.p.)
2. 4.65
3. 81
4. £440

Page 80 – Averages 2

A

1. c
2. b
3. a
4. a

B

1. 21.5 mm
2. a) mode 47
   b) median 35
   c) range 40

C

1. 1 | 2 4 9 5 7 8 8 5
   2 | 2 7 3 5 7 7
   3 | 1 6 5 2 8
   4 | 1
   Reordering gives:
   1 | 2 4 5 5 7 8 8 9
   2 | 2 3 5 7 7 7
   3 | 1 2 5 6 8
   4 | 1
   Key: 1|2 means 12 minutes
   Stem: 10 minutes
2. a) £31.80
   b) This is only an estimate because the midpoints of the data has been used.
   c) $30 \leq x < 40$

Page 82 – Probability 1

A

1. c
2. d
3. c
4. b
5. a

B

1. a) $\frac{2}{11}$
   b) $\frac{2}{11}$
   c) $\frac{3}{11}$
   d) 0
2. 0.4
3. a) true
   b) false
   c) false
4. 100 students

C

1.

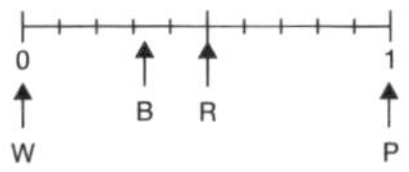

2. a) i) $\frac{5}{20} = \frac{1}{4}$
   ii) $\frac{7}{20}$
   b) $\frac{16}{20} = \frac{4}{5}$
3. a) i) 0.35
   ii) 0
   b) 50 times

Page 84 – Probability 2

A

1. c
2. a
3. a
4. d

B

1. a)

Spinner 2 \ Spinner 1	1	2	3	3
1	2	**3**	**4**	**4**
2	**3**	**4**	5	5
3	**4**	5	**6**	**6**
6	**7**	8	9	**9**

   b) i) $\frac{4}{16} = \frac{1}{4}$
   ii) $\frac{2}{16} = \frac{1}{8}$
   iii) 0
2. HO, HT, CO, CT, BO, BT
   (H = Ham, C = Cheese, B = Beef, O = Orange, T = Tea)
3. 0.7

C

1. a) $\frac{6}{36} = \frac{1}{6}$
   b) $\frac{4}{36} = \frac{1}{9}$
2. a)

	Under 13 years old	13 years and over	Total
Boys	15	**27**	42
Girls	**12**	21	**33**
Total	**27**	**48**	75

   b) $\frac{27}{75} = \frac{9}{25}$
3. SS, SF, TS, TF, AS, AF

ACKNOWLEDGEMENTS

The author and publisher are grateful to the copyright holders for permission to use quoted materials and images.

Letts Educational
4 Grosvenor Place
London SW1X 7DL

School orders: 015395 64910
School enquiries: 015395 65921
Parent and student enquiries: 015395 64913
Email: enquiries@lettsandlonsdale.co.uk
Website: www.lettsandlonsdale.com

British Library Cataloguing in Publication Data. A CIP record of this book is available from the British Library.

This material has been endorsed by Edexcel and offers high quality support for the delivery of Edexcel qualifications.

Edexcel endorsement does not mean that this material is essential to achieve any Edexcel qualification, nor does it mean that this is the only suitable material available to support any Edexcel qualification. No endorsed material will be used verbatim in setting any Edexcel examination and any resource lists produced by Edexcel shall include this and other appropriate texts. While this material has been through an Edexcel quality assurance process, all responsibility for the content remains with the publisher.

Copies of official specifications for all Edexcel qualifications may be found on the Edexcel website - www.edexcel.org.uk

Book concept and development: Helen Jacobs
Author: Fiona C. Mapp
Editorial: Marion Davies, Alan Worth
Project Editor: Charlotte Christensen
Cover design: Angela English
Inside concept design: Starfish Design
Text design, layout and editorial: Servis Filmsetting, Letts & Lonsdale

Printed and bound in Italy

Letts and Lonsdale make every effort to ensure that all paper used in our books is made from wood pulp obtained from sustainable and well-managed forests, controlled sources and recycled wood or fibre.

C

These are GCSE-style questions. Answer all parts of the questions. Show your workings (on separate paper if necessary) and include the correct units in your answers.

1 Write down the mathematical name of each of these 3D shapes. (2 marks)

a)

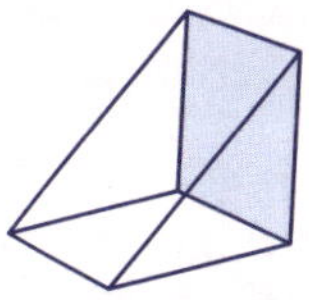

....

b)

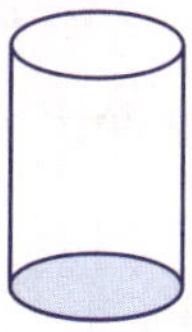

....

2 Sketch a net of this 3D shape. (3 marks)

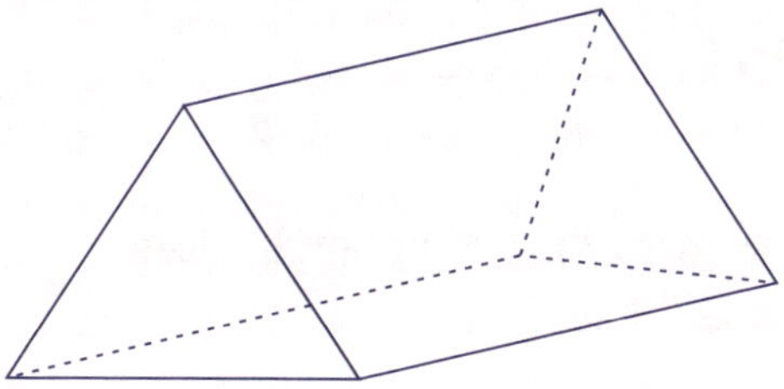

3 The diagram shows a model made up from 1 cm cubes

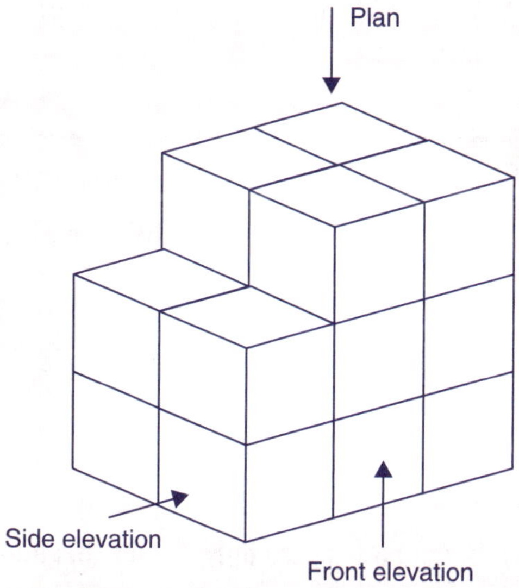

In the space provided, draw a sketch of:

a) the plan

b) the front elevation

c) the side elevation of the model. (3 marks)

Score /8

How well did you do?
1–5 Try again 6–9 Getting there 10–14 Good work 15–20 Excellent!

For more information on this topic see pages 50–51 of your Success Guide.

Symmetry and constructions

A Choose just one answer, a, b, c or d.

Questions 1–5 relate to these diagrams.

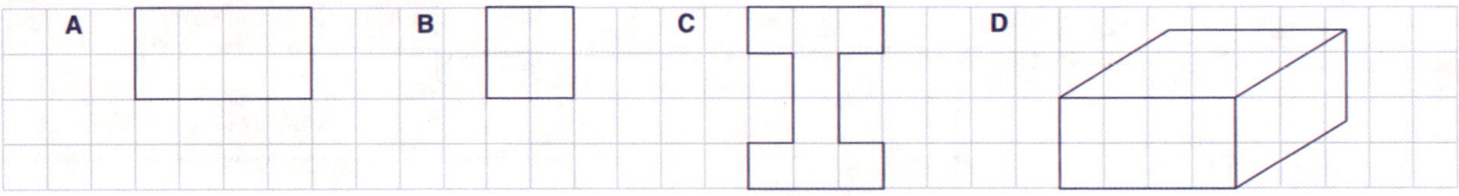

1 What is the order of rotational symmetry of shape B? (1 mark)

a) 4 b) 2 c) 3 d) 1

2 How many planes of symmetry does shape D have? (1 mark)

a) 5 b) 4 c) 2 d) 3

3 How many lines of symmetry does shape B have? (1 mark)

a) 4 b) 3 c) 2 d) 1

4 What is the order of rotational symmetry of shape C? (1 mark)

a) 1 b) 3 c) 2 d) 4

5 How many lines of symmetry does shape C have? (1 mark)

a) 4 b) 2 c) 3 d) 1

Score / 5

B Answer all parts of the questions.

1 Draw in one plane of symmetry on each of the solids below. (4 marks)

a)

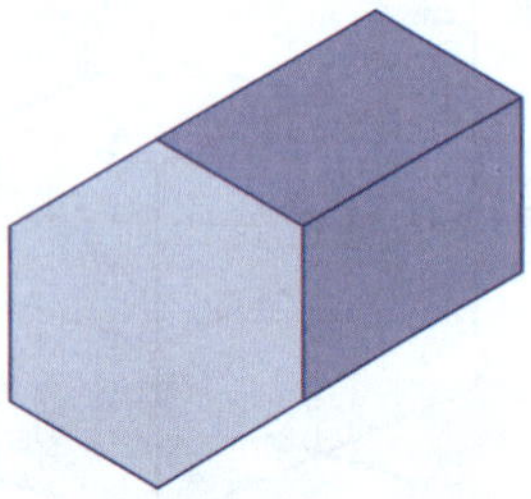

b)

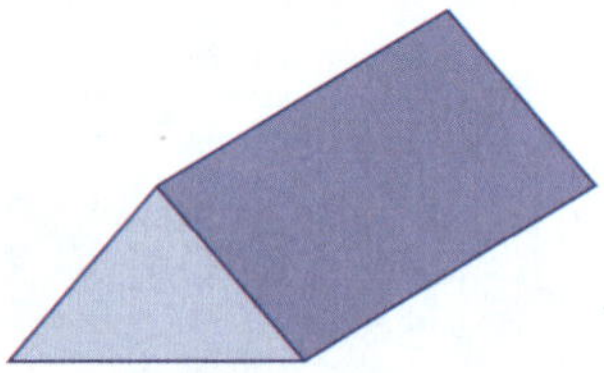

2 a) Using compasses only, bisect this angle. (2 marks)

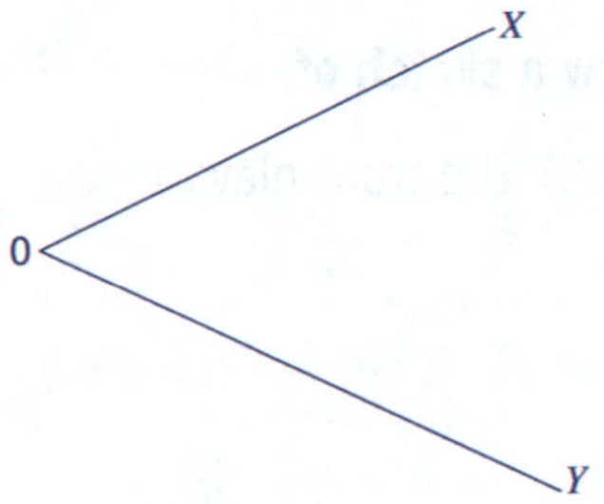

b) Measure angle XOY. (1 mark)

....

3 On a separate piece of paper, using ruler and compasses only, make an accurate drawing of this triangle. (3 marks)

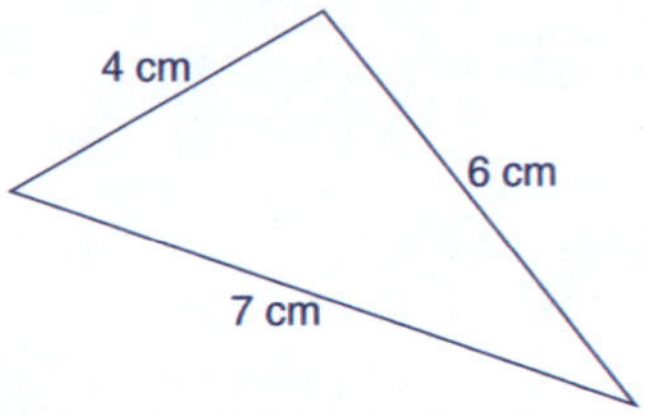

Score / 10

C

These are GCSE-style questions. Answer all parts of the questions. Show your workings (on separate paper if necessary) and include the correct units in your answers.

1 a) Draw the lines of symmetry on the rectangle below. (2 marks)

b) What is the order of rotational symmetry of the rectangle? (1 mark)

....

2 The diagram shows a prism. Draw one plane of symmetry of the prism on the diagram. (2 marks)

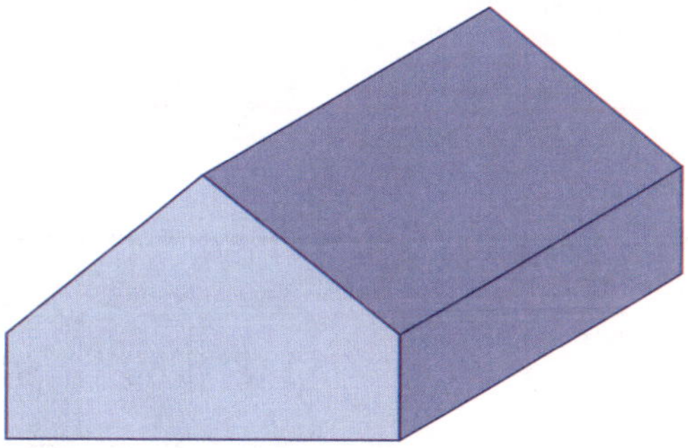

3 Showing construction lines, draw accurately the perpendicular bisector of this line. (2 marks)

Score /7

How well did you do? 1–6 Try again 7–11 Getting there 12–17 Good work 18–22 Excellent!

For more information on this topic see pages 52–55 of your Success Guide.

Angles

A Choose just one answer, a, b, c or d.

1 What is the name given to an angle of size 72°? (1 mark)

a) acute b) obtuse
c) reflex d) right angle

2 When shapes tessellate, the angles at the point at which they meet add up to this angle. (1 mark)

a) 180° b) 90°
c) 360° d) 270°

3 Two angles in a scalene triangle are 104° and 39°. What is the size of the third angle? (1 mark)

a) 217° b) 37°
c) 57° d) 157°

4 In the diagram below, what is the size of angle a? (1 mark)

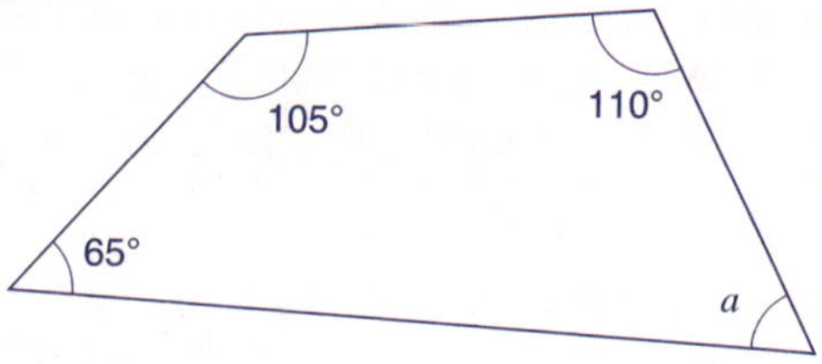

a) 90° b) 80°
c) 75° d) 100°

5 The size of the exterior angle of a regular polygon is 20°. How many sides does the polygon have? (1 mark)

a) 18 b) 15
c) 10 d) 20

Score / 5

B Answer all parts of the questions.

1 Here are the sizes of some angles, written on cards.

148° | 60° | 91° | 63° | 154° | 65° | 68°

Match the correct card to the missing angle n in each of the diagrams.

a)

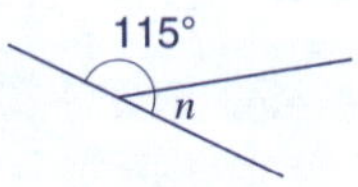

n = ...

(1 mark)

b)

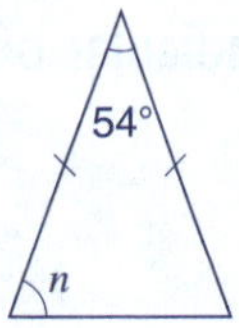

n = ...

(1 mark)

c)

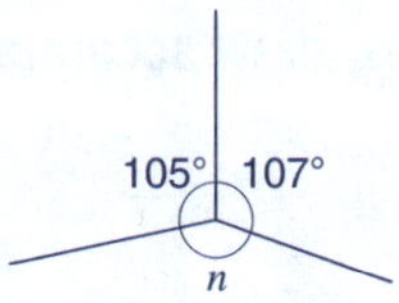

n = ...

(1 mark)

d)

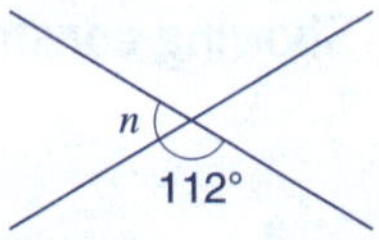

n = ...

(1 mark)

e)

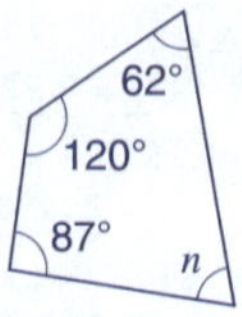

n = ...

(1 mark)

f)

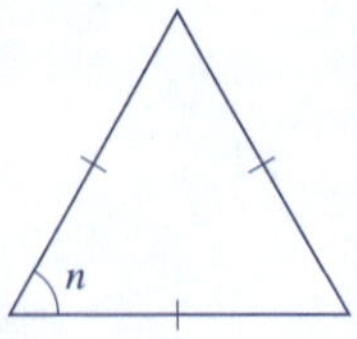

n = ...

(1 mark)

g)

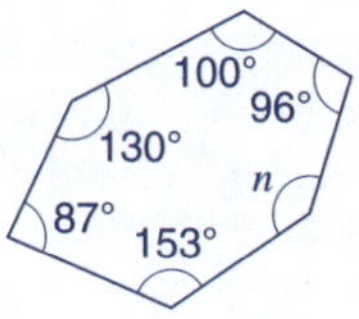

n = ...

(2 marks)

2 On the grid, draw six more shapes to continue this tessellation.

(2 marks)

Score / 10

C

These are GCSE-style questions. Answer all parts of the questions. Show your workings (on separate paper if necessary) and include the correct units in your answers.

1 In the diagram, AB is vertical and BDE is a horizontal straight line.

BC = BD, CF is parallel to BDE.

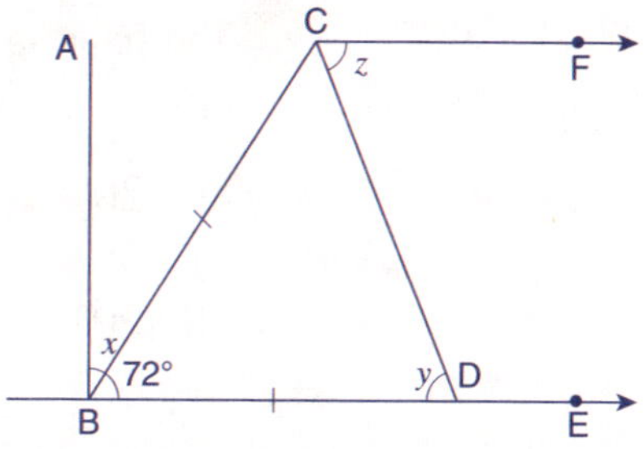

a) i) Work out the size of the angle marked x°. (2 marks)

.... °

ii) Give a reason for your answer. (2 marks)

....

....

b) i) Work out the size of the angle marked y°.

.... °

ii) Give a reason for your answer. (2 marks)

....

....

c) i) Work out the size of the angle marked z°. (2 marks)

.... °

ii) Give a reason for your answer.

....

....

2 The diagram shows a hexagon.

Find the size of the angle marked x°. (4 marks)

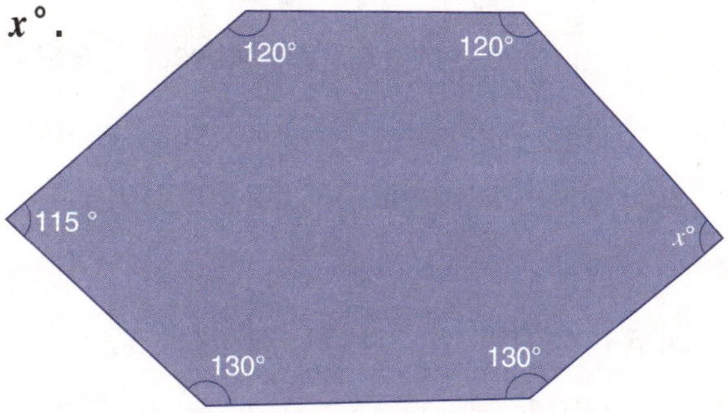

.... °

Score / 12

How well did you do? ✗ 1–7 Try again 8–13 Getting there 14–21 Good work 22–27 Excellent! ✓

For more information on this topic see pages 54–55 & 49 of your Success Guide.

Bearings and scale drawings

A

Choose just one answer, a, b, c or d.

1 **The bearing of P from Q is 050°. What is the bearing of Q from P?** (1 mark)

a) 130°
b) 50°
c) 230°
d) 310°

2 **The bearing of R from S is 130°. What is the bearing of S from R?** (1 mark)

a) 310°
b) 230°
c) 050°
d) 200°

3 **The bearing of A from B is 240°. What is the bearing of B from A?** (1 mark)

a) 120°
b) 60°
c) 320°
d) 060°

4 **The length of a car park is 25 metres. A scale diagram of the car park is being drawn to a scale of 1 cm to 5 metres. What is the length of the car park on the scale diagram?** (1 mark)

a) 500 mm
b) 5 cm
c) 50 cm
d) 5 m

Score / 4

B

Answer all parts of the questions.

1 **The scale on a road map is 1 : 50 000. Two towns are 20 cm apart on the map. Work out the real distance, in km, between them.** (2 marks)

.... km

2 **A ship sails on a bearing of 065° for 10 km. It then continues on a bearing of 120° for a further 15 km to a port (P).**

a) On a separate piece of paper, draw, using a scale of 1 cm to 2 km, an accurate scale drawing of this information. (3 marks)

b) Measure on your diagram the direct distance between the start and the port (P). (1 mark)

.... km

c) What is the bearing of port P from the starting point? (1 mark)

.... °

3 'The bearing of B from A is 060°.' (1 mark)

Is this statement true or false?

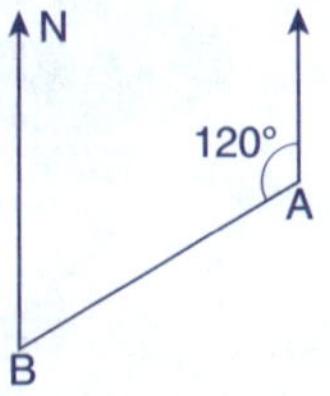

....

Score / 8

C

These are GCSE-style questions. Answer all parts of the questions. Show your workings (on separate paper if necessary) and include the correct units in your answers.

1

Scale: 1cm represents 50m

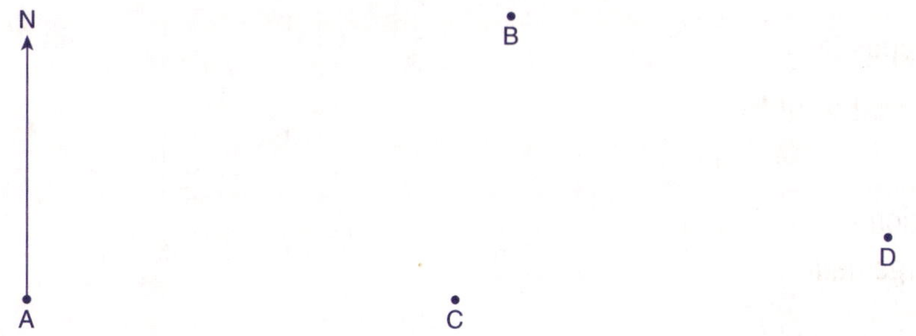

The scale drawing shows the positions of points A, B, C and D. Point C is due east of point A.

a) Use measurements from the drawing to find:

i) the distance, in metres, of B from A .... m (1 mark)

ii) the bearing of B from A .... ° (2 marks)

iii) the bearing of D from B .... ° (2 marks)

b) Point E is 250 m from C on a bearing of 055°. Mark the position of point E on the diagram above. (2 marks)

2 **Here is a sketch of a triangle.**

Use a compass and a ruler to make an accurate scale drawing of the triangle. (3 marks)

Use a scale of 1 cm to 2 m

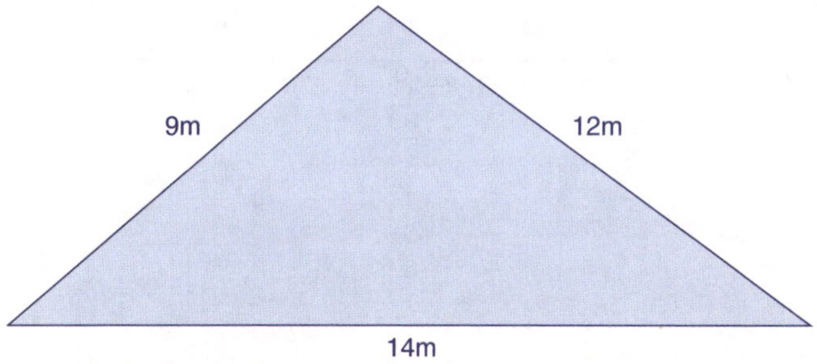

Score / 10

How well did you do? 1–5 Try again 6–10 Getting there 11–17 Good work 18–22 Excellent!

For more information on this topic see pages 56–57 of your Success Guide.

Transformations 1

A

Choose just one answer, a, b, c or d.

Questions 1–4 refer to the artwork opposite.

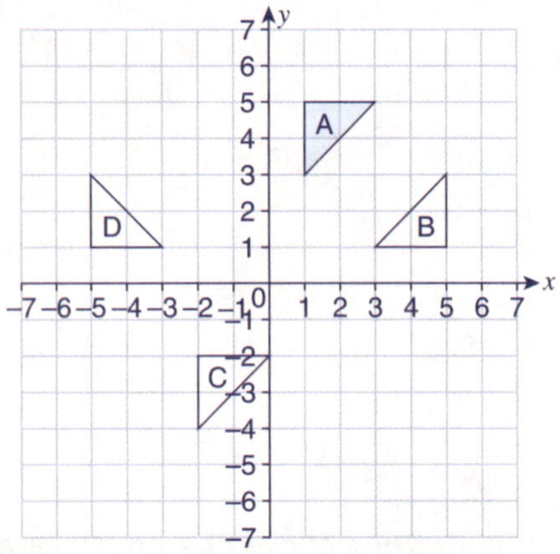

1 What is the single transformation that would map shape A onto shape B? (1 mark)

a) reflection b) rotation
c) translation d) enlargement

2 What is the single transformation that would map shape A onto shape C? (1 mark)

a) reflection b) rotation
c) translation d) enlargement

3 What is the single transformation that would map shape A onto shape D? (1 mark)

a) reflection b) rotation
c) translation d) enlargement

4 What special name is given to the relationship between the triangles A, B, C and D? (1 mark)

a) enlargement b) congruent
c) translation d) similar

Score / 4

B

Answer all parts of the questions.

1 On the grid, carry out the following transformations. (3 marks)

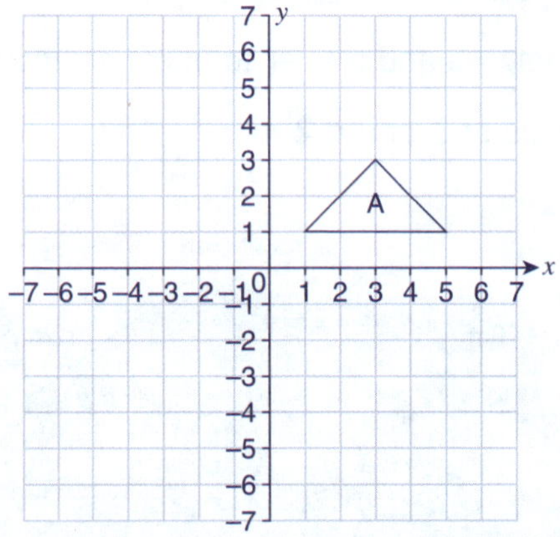

a) Reflect shape A in the *y* axis.
Call the new shape R.

b) Rotate shape A 90° clockwise, about (0, 0).
Call the new shape S.

c) Translate shape A by the vector $\begin{pmatrix} -3 \\ 4 \end{pmatrix}$
Call the new shape T.

2 All the following shapes are either a reflection, rotation or translation of object P. State the single transformation that has taken place for each of the following. (4 marks)

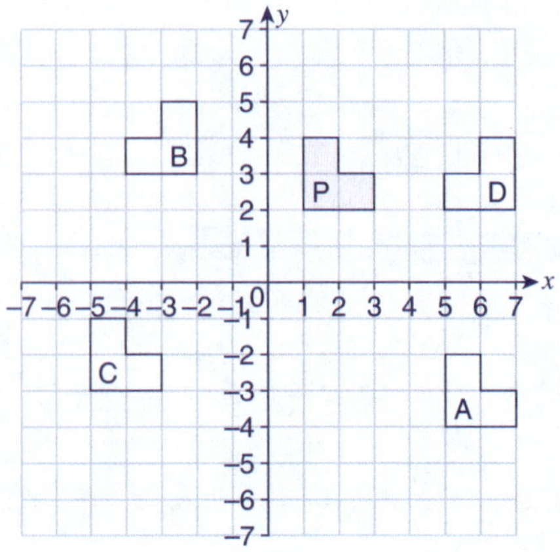

a) P is transformed to A. ....

b) P is transformed to B. ....

c) P is transformed to C. ....

d) P is transformed to D. ....

Score / 7

C

These are GCSE-style questions. Answer all parts of the questions. Show your workings (on separate paper if necessary) and include the correct units in your answers.

1

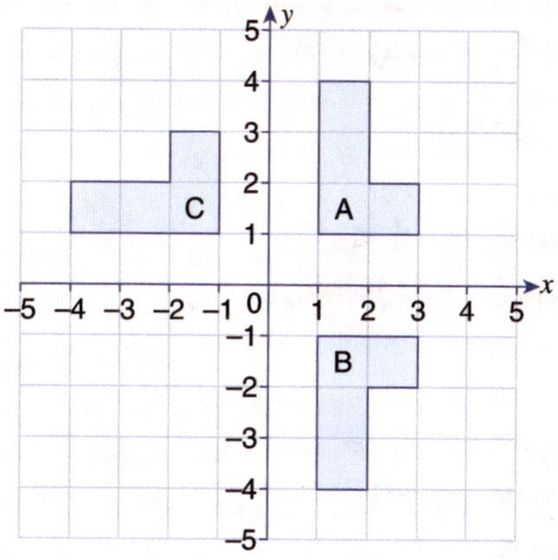

a) Describe fully the single transformation which maps shape A onto shape B. (2 marks)

....

....

b) Describe fully the single transformation which maps shape A onto shape C. (3 marks)

....

....

2

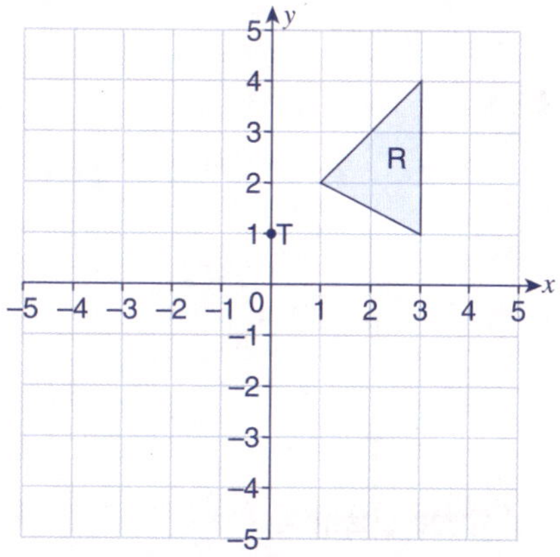

The triangle R has been drawn on the grid.

a) Rotate triangle R 90° clockwise about the point T (0, 1) and call the image P. (3 marks)

b) Translate triangle R by the vector $\begin{pmatrix} -4 \\ -3 \end{pmatrix}$ and call the image Q. (3 marks)

Score / 11

How well did you do? ✗ 1–6 Try again 7–10 Getting there 11–16 Good work 17–22 Excellent! ✓

For more information on this topic see pages 58–59 of your Success Guide.

Transformations 2

A Choose just one answer, a, b, c or d.

Questions 1–3 refer to the diagram opposite.

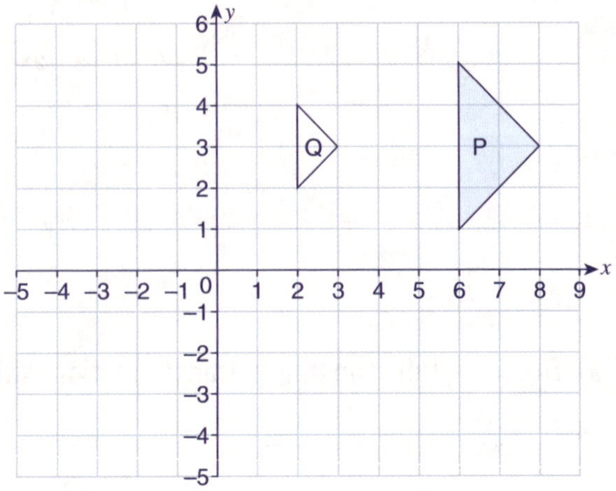

1 **Shape P is enlarged to give shape Q. What is the scale factor of the enlargement?** (1 mark)

a) $\frac{1}{3}$ b) 2
c) 3 d) $\frac{1}{2}$

2 **Shape Q is enlarged to give shape P. What is the scale factor of the enlargement?** (1 mark)

a) $\frac{1}{3}$ b) 2 c) 3 d) $\frac{1}{2}$

3 **What are the coordinates of the centre of enlargement?** (1 mark)

a) (3, −2) b) (−2, 3)
c) (−3, 4) d) (0, 0)

Score / 3

B Answer all parts of the questions.

1 **Draw an enlargement of shape R, with centre O and scale factor 3. Call the image P.** (3 marks)

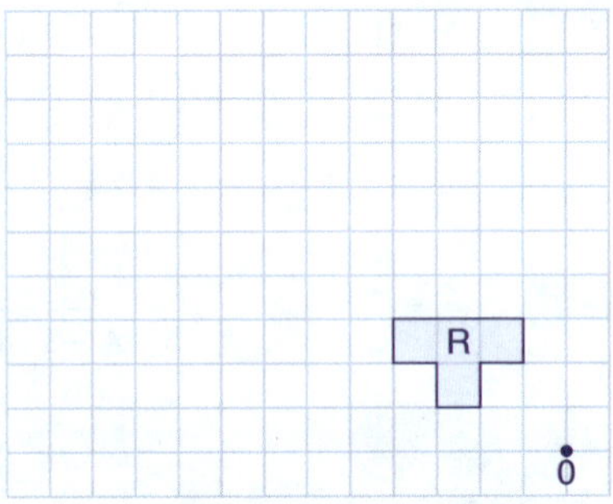

2 **The diagram shows the position of three shapes, A, B and C.**

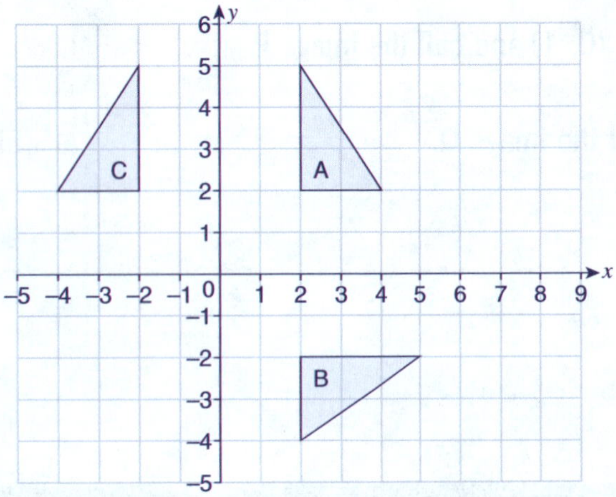

a) Describe the transformation which moves A onto C. (2 marks)

....

....

b) Describe the transformation which moves A onto B. (2 marks)

....

....

c) Describe the transformation which moves B onto C. (2 marks)

....

....

Score / 9

C These are GCSE-style questions. Answer all parts of the questions. Show your workings (on separate paper if necessary) and include the correct units in your answers.

1 a) Draw an enlargement of the shape.

Use a scale factor of 2.

Call the enlarged shape A. (2 marks)

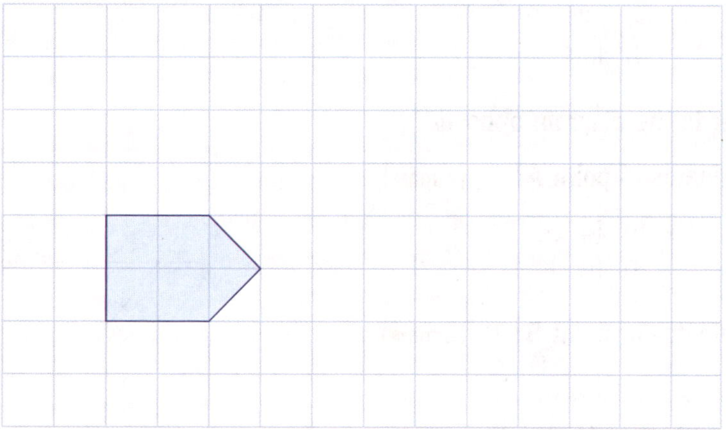

b) If the area of the original shape is 5 cm², what is the area of the enlarged shape? (1 mark)

.... cm²

2 Enlarge triangle N by a scale factor of $\frac{1}{3}$ with centre R (−6, 7). (3 marks)

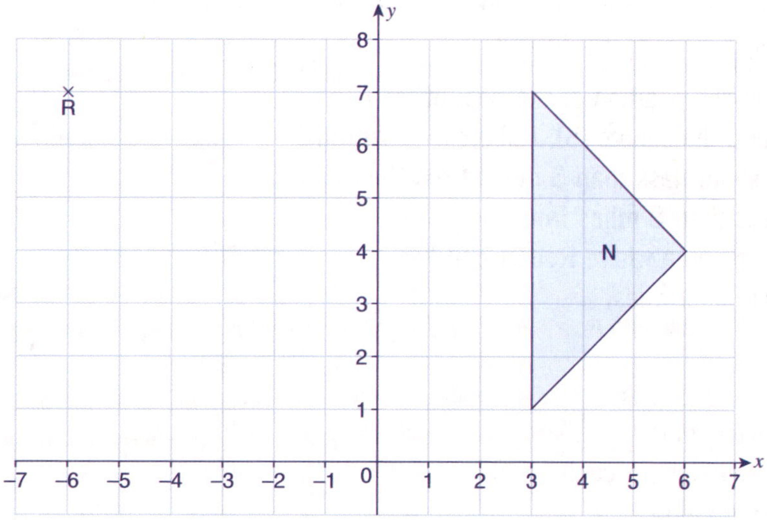

Score /6

How well did you do? 1–3 Try again 4–8 Getting there 9–13 Good work 14–18 Excellent!

For more information on this topic see pages 59–61 of your Success Guide.

Loci and coordinates

A

Choose just one answer, a, b, c or d.

1 **What shape would be formed if the locus of all the points from a fixed point P is drawn?** (1 mark)

a) rectangle b) square
c) circle d) kite

2 **Questions 2–5 refer to the diagram opposite.**

What are the coordinates of point A? (1 mark)

a) (4, 3, 1) b) (4, 3, 0)
c) (0, 3, 1) d) (0, 1, 4)

3 **What are the coordinates of point B?** (1 mark)

a) (3, 1, 0) b) (0, 0, 0)
c) (4, 3, 0) d) (0, 3, 0)

4 **What are the coordinates of point C?** (1 mark)

a) (0, 3, 1) b) (4, 3, 1)
c) (4, 0, 0) d) (3, 0, 4)

5 **What are the coordinates of point D?** (1 mark)

a) (4, 3, 0) b) (3, 1, 4)
c) (0, 0, 0) d) (0, 3, 0)

Score / 5

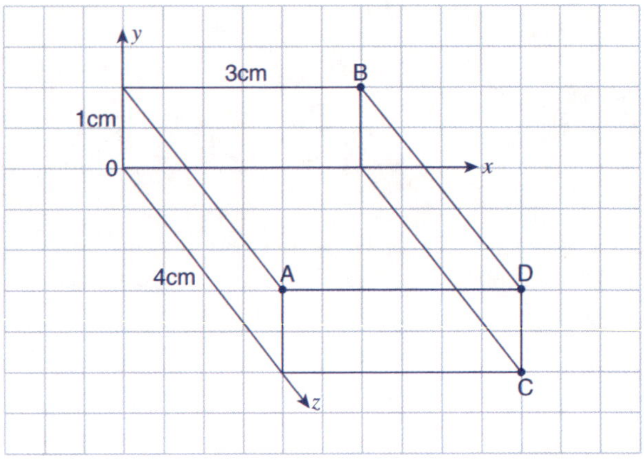

B

Answer all parts of the questions.

1 **The diagram shows the position of the post office (P), the hospital (H) and the school (S). Robert lives within 4 miles of the hospital, less than 5 miles from the post office and less than 8 miles from the school. Show by shading the area where Robert can live. Use a scale of 1 cm = 2 miles.** (4 marks)

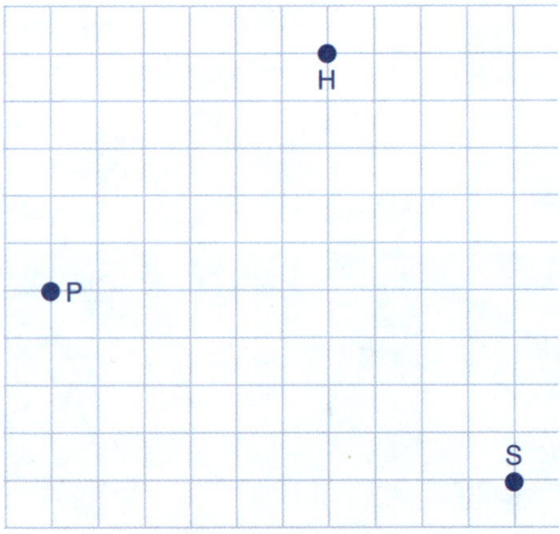

2 **The diagram shows a solid. Complete the coordinates for each of the vertices listed below.** (4 marks)

R = (.... , ... , ...)

S = (.... , ... , ...)

T = (.... , ... , ...)

U = (.... , ... , ...)

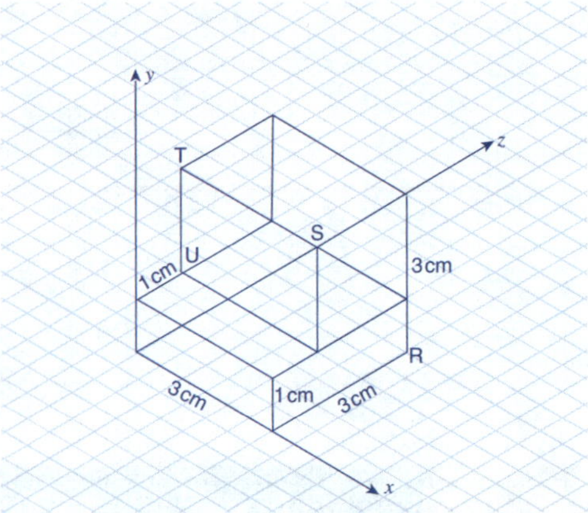

Score / 8

C These are GCSE-style questions. Answer all parts of the questions. Show your workings (on separate paper if necessary) and include the correct units in your answers.

1 In this question you should only use ruler and compasses for the constructions.

Triangle ABC is an adventure playground, drawn to a scale of 1 cm to 20 m.

a) On the diagram, draw accurately the locus of the points which are 100 m from C. (2 marks)

b) On the diagram, draw accurately the locus of the points which are the same distance from A as they are from C. (2 marks)

c) P is an ice cream kiosk inside the adventure playground.

P is the same distance from A as it is from C.

P is the same distance from AC as it is from AB.

On the diagram, mark the point P clearly with a cross.

Label it with the letter P. (3 marks)

2 A cuboid lies on the coordinate axes.

The point R has coordinates (5,4,3).

Write down the coordinates of point S. (1 mark)

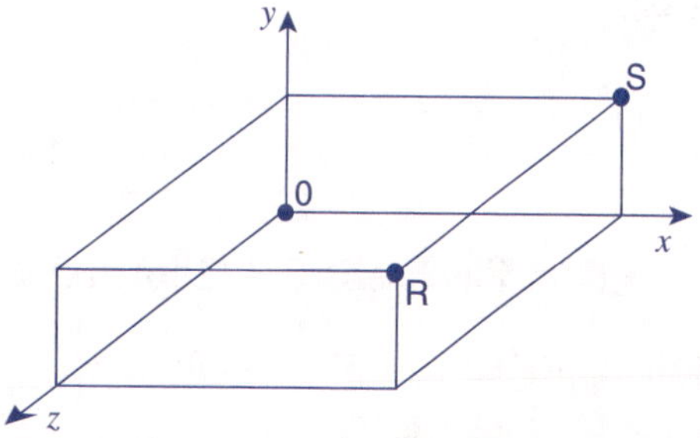

....

Score /8

How well did you do? 1–4 Try again 5–9 Getting there 10–14 Good work 15–21 Excellent!

For more information on this topic see page 62–63 of your Success Guide.

Pythagoras' theorem

A

Choose just one answer, a, b, c or d.

1 **What is the name of the longest side of a right-angled triangle?** (1 mark)

a) hypo b) hippopotamus
c) crocodile d) hypotenuse

2 **Calculate the missing length y of this triangle.** (C)

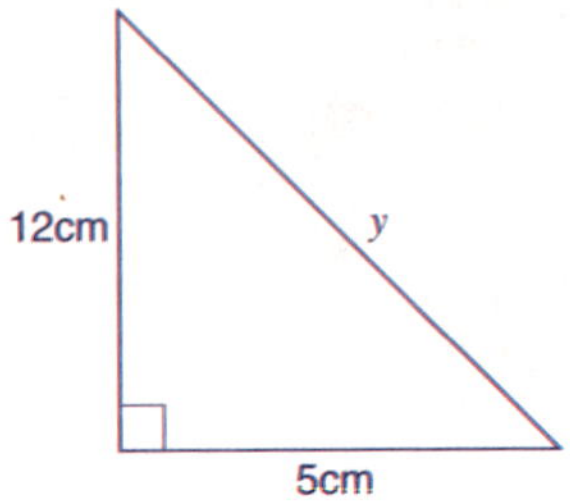

a) 169 cm b) 13 cm (1 mark)
c) 17 cm d) 84.5 cm

3 **Calculate the missing length y of this triangle.**

a) 13.2 cm b) 5 cm (C) (1 mark)
c) 25 cm d) 625 cm

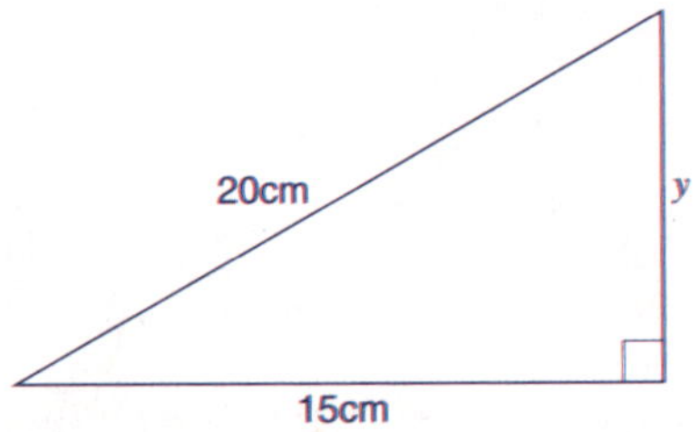

4 **Point A has coordinates (1, 4), point B has coordinates (4, 10). What are the coordinates of the midpoint of the line AB?** (1 mark)

a) (5, 14) b) (3, 6)
c) (2.5, 7) d) (1.5, 3)

Score / 4

B

Answer all parts of the questions.

1 **Calculate the missing lengths of these right-angled triangles. Give your answers to 3 significant figures, where appropriate.** (C)

a)

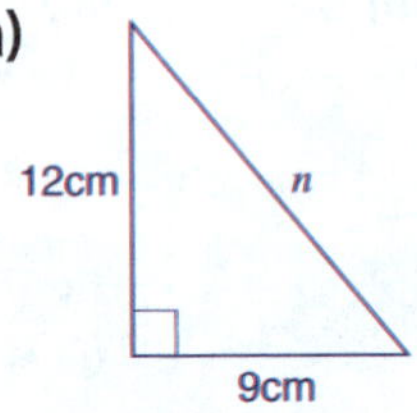

$n =$ ....cm (2 marks)

b)

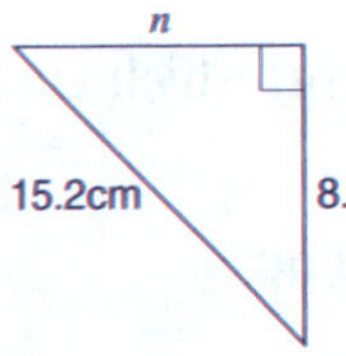

$n =$ ....cm (2 marks)

c)

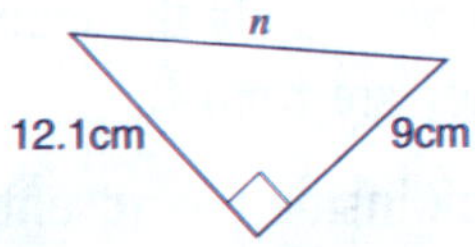

$n =$ ....cm (2 marks)

d)

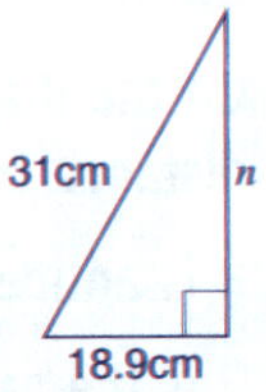

$n =$ ....cm (2 marks)

2 **Molly says, 'The angle x in this triangle is 90°.'**

Explain how Molly knows this without measuring the size of the angle. (2 marks)

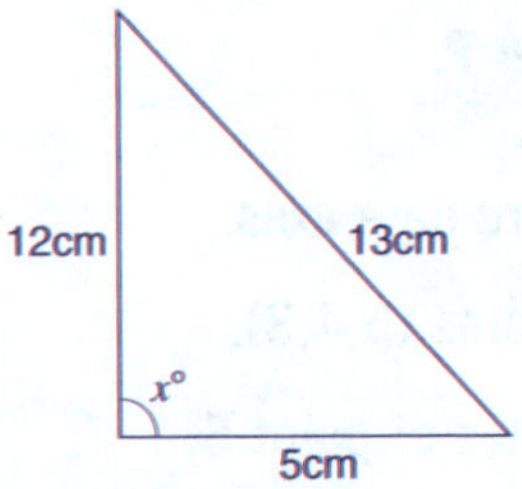

....

....

3 **Colin says, 'The length of this line is 6.7 (1dp) and the coordinates of the midpoint are (3.5, 8).'**

Decide whether these statements are true or false.
Give an explanation for your answer. (2 marks)

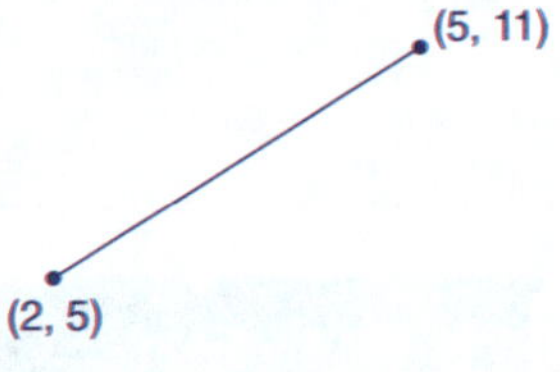

....

....

Score / 12

(C) *Indicates that a calculator may be used*

C

These are GCSE-style questions. Answer all parts of the questions. Show your workings (on separate paper if necessary) and include the correct units in your answers.

1 ABC is a right-angled triangle.

AB = 5 cm, BC = 6 cm. (C)

Calculate the length of AC.

Give your answer to one decimal place.

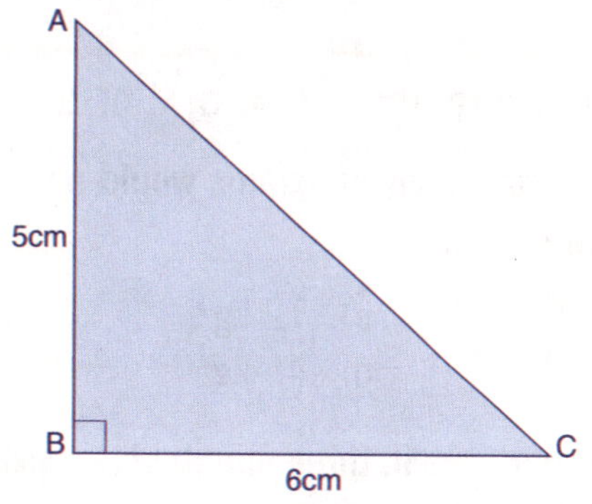

(3 marks)

.... cm

2 Calculate the length of the diagonal of this rectangle.
Give your answer to one decimal place. (C)

(3 marks)

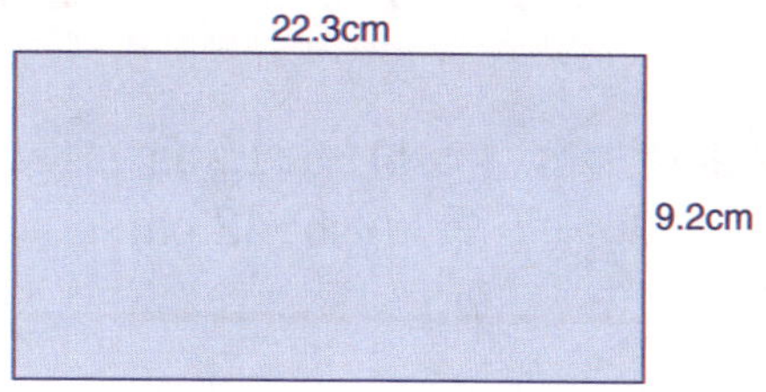

.... cm

3 Calculate the perpendicular height of the isosceles triangle.
Give your answer to one decimal place. (C)

(3 marks)

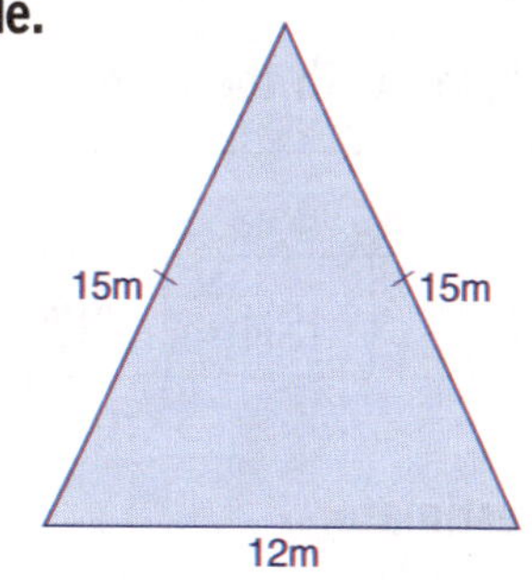

.... cm

4 Calculate the length of AB in this diagram.
Give your answer to one decimal place.

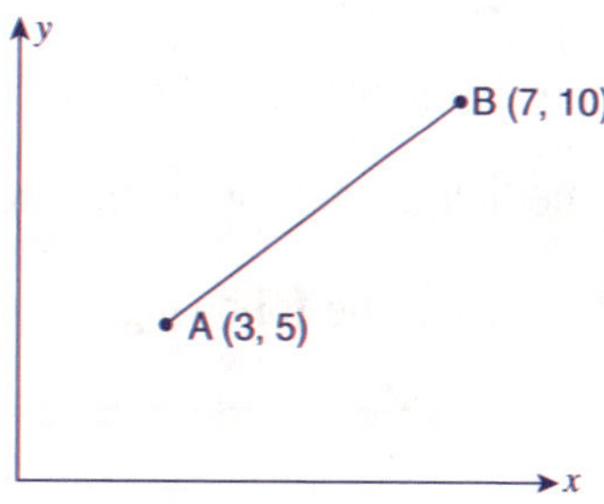

(3 marks)

Diagram not drawn to scale

.... cm

Score / 12

How well did you do? 1–7 Try again 8–14 Getting there 15–21 Good work 22–28 Excellent!

For more information on this topic see pages 64–65 of your Success Guide.

Measures and measurement 1

A

Choose just one answer, a, b, c or d.

1 **Approximately how many kilograms would an 'average' man weigh?** (1 mark)

a) 720 kg b) 72 kg
c) 7.2 kg d) 45 kg

2 **How many seconds are in three minutes?** (1 mark)

a) 180 b) 60
c) 240 d) 120

3 **What is 1842 written as a 12-hour time?** (1 mark)

a) 6 : 42 am b) 6 : 15 am
c) 6 : 42 d) 6 : 42 pm

4 **What is 5:25 am written in 24-hour time?** (1 mark)

a) 5:25 pm b) 0525 am
c) 0525 pm d) 0525

5 **How many days are there in a leap year?** (1 mark)

a) 366 b) 364
c) 365 d) 367

Score / 5

B

Answer all parts of the questions.

1 **Complete the table below with the correct times.** (2 marks)

12-hour clock	4:23 pm			3:16 pm		9:38 pm
24-hour clock		1534	2126		0314	

2 **Using metric units, estimate:**

a) the length of your classroom .... (1 mark)

b) the distance from Manchester to London .... (1 mark)

c) the volume of medicine on a medicine spoon .... (1 mark)

3 **On the scales below, mark the following readings.** (4 marks)

a) 6.7

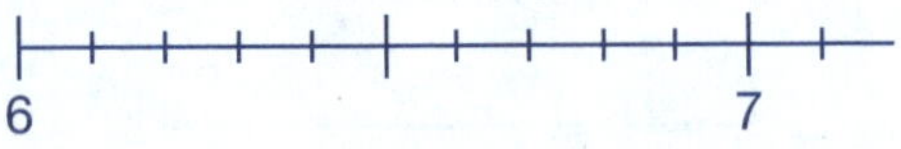

b) 9.4

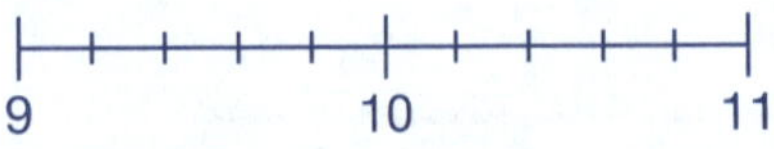

c) 12.75

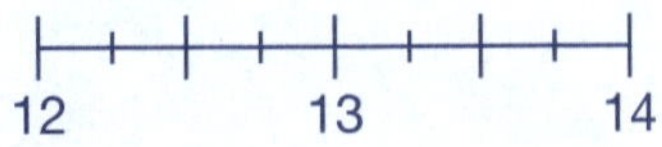

d) 7.34

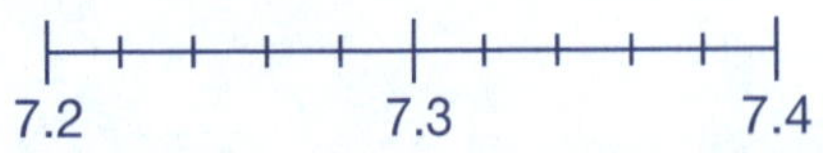

Score / 9

C

These are GCSE-style questions. Answer all parts of the questions. Show your workings (on separate paper if necessary) and include the correct units in your answers.

1 **a) Write down the number marked with an arrow on this meter.** (1 mark)

....

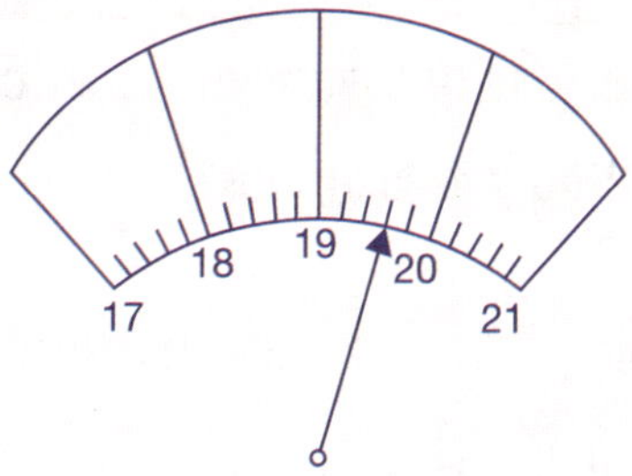

b) Write down the number marked with an arrow on this scale. (1 mark)

....

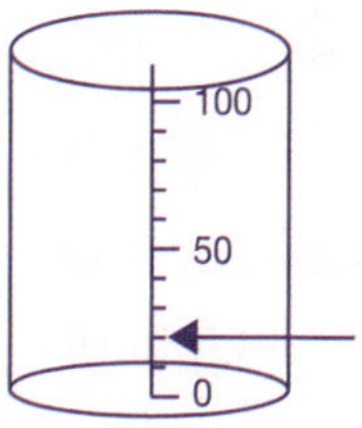

c) Find the number 16 on the number line. Mark it with an arrow (↑). (1 mark)

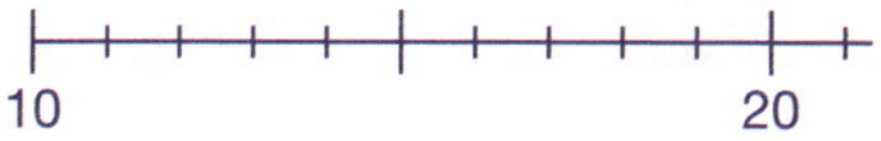

d) Find the number 12.4 on the number line. Mark it with an arrow (↑). (1 mark)

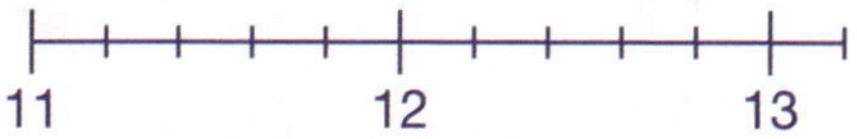

2 This is part of the timetable for Jessica's day.

8:45	Registration
9:05	Maths begins
9:55	Maths ends and English begins
10:45	English ends and break begins
11:00	Break ends and Art begins
11:50	Art ends and Science begins
12:40	Science ends and lunch begins.

a) How long is registration? .... (1 mark)

b) How long does the Art lesson last? .... (1 mark)

c) A fire alarm went off at 10:23 am. How many minutes was this before break? (1 mark)

....

d) Matthew was late for school. He arrived at 9:36 am. How many minutes late was he? (1 mark)

....

Score / 8

How well did you do? ✗ 1–6 Try again 7–11 Getting there 12–16 Good work 17–22 Excellent! ✓

For more information on this topic see pages 66–68 of your Success Guide.

Measures and measurement 2

A

Choose just one answer, a, b, c or d.

1 What is 2500 g in kilograms? (1 mark)

a) 25 kg b) 2.5 kg
c) 0.25 kg d) 250 kg

2 Approximately how many pounds are in 4 kg? (1 mark)

a) 6.9 b) 12.4
c) 7.7 d) 8.8

3 Jessica is 165 cm tall to the nearest cm. What is the lower limit of her height? (1 mark)

a) 164.5 cm b) 165.5 cm
c) 165 cm d) 164.9 cm

4 What is the volume of a piece of wood with a density of 680 kg/m^3 and a mass of 34 kg? (C) (1 mark)

a) 0.5 m^3 b) 20 m^3
c) 2 m^3 d) 0.05 m^3

5 A car travels for two and a half hours at an average speed of 42 mph. How far does the car travel? (C) (1 mark)

a) 96 miles b) 100 miles
c) 105 miles d) 140 miles

Score / 5

B

Answer all parts of the questions.

1 Complete the statements below. (6 marks)

a) 8 km = ………………… m b) 3250 g = ………………… kg
c) 7 tonnes = ………………… kg d) 52 cm = ………………… m
e) 2.7 l = ………………… ml e) 262 cm = ………………… km

2 Two towns are approximately 20 km apart. How many miles is this? (C) (1 mark)

……………………………………………………………………………………………

3 A recipe uses 600 g of flour. Approximately how many pounds is this? (C) (1 mark)

……………………………………………………………………………………………

4 A field is 47 metres long to the nearest metre. Write down the upper and lower limits of the length of the field. (2 marks)

……………………………………………………………………………………………

5 Giovanni drove 200 miles in 3 hours and 45 minutes. At what average speed did he travel? (C) (2 marks)

……………………………………………………………………………………………

6 What is the density of a toy if its mass is 200 g and its volume is 2000 cm^3? (2 marks)

……………………………………………………………………………………………

Score / 14

(C) *Indicates that a calculator may be used*

C

These are GCSE-style questions. Answer all parts of the questions. Show your workings (on separate paper if necessary) and include the correct units in your answers.

1 a) Change 8 kilograms into pounds. (C) b) Change 30 miles into kilometres. (2 marks)

.... pounds .... kilometres (2 marks)

2 Two solids each have a volume of $2.5m^3$.

The density of solid A is 320 kg per m^3.

The density of solid B is 288 kg per m^3.

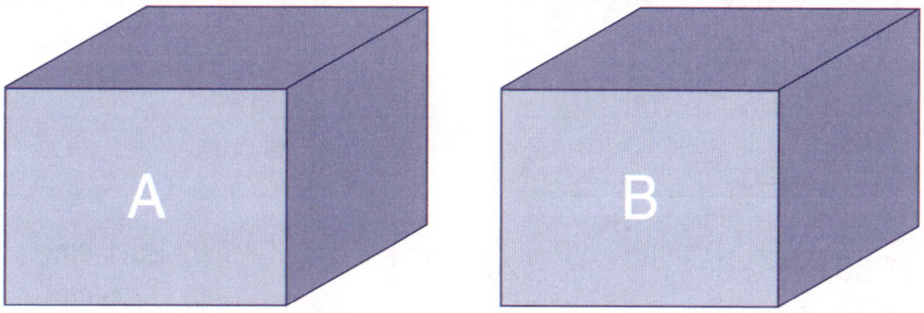

Calculate the difference between the masses of the solids. (C)

.... kg (3 marks)

3 Amy took part in a sponsored walk.

She walked from the school to the park and back.

The distance from the school to the park is 8 km.

a) Amy walked from the school to the park at an average speed of 5 km/h.

Find the time she took to walk from the school to the park. (C) (2 marks)

....

b) Her average speed for the return journey was 4 km/h.

Calculate her average speed for the whole journey. (C) (4 marks)

....

4 The length of the rectangle is 12.1 cm to the nearest mm.

The width of the rectangle is 6 cm to the nearest cm.

Write down the lower limits for the length and width of the rectangle.

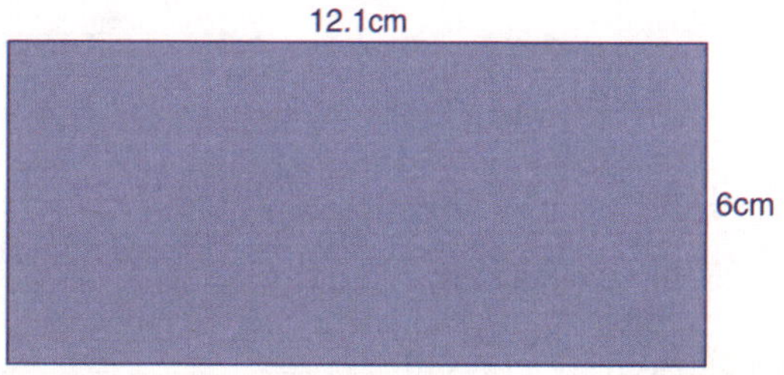

Length .... cm (2 marks)

Width .... cm

5 A book has a mass of 112 grams, correct to the nearest gram. (2 marks)

a) Write down the least possible mass of the book .... grams

b) Write down the greatest possible mass of the book .... grams

Score / 17

How well did you do? 1–11 Try again 12–19 Getting there 20–27 Good work 28–36 Excellent!

For more information on this topic see pages 66–69 of your Success Guide.

Area of 2D shapes

A Choose just one answer, a, b, c or d.

1 What is the area of this triangle? (1 mark)

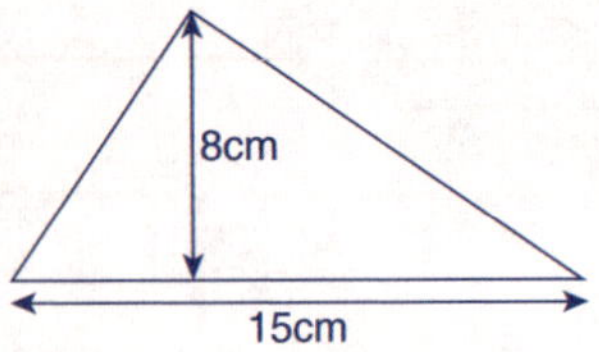

a) $60\ mm^2$ b) $120\ cm^2$
c) $60\ cm^2$ d) $46\ cm^2$

2 What is the approximate circumference of a circle of radius 4 cm? (1 mark)

a) $25.1\ cm^2$ b) 50.3 cm
c) 12.6 cm d) 25.1 cm

3 Change $50\,000\ cm^2$ into m^2. (1 mark)

a) $500\ m^2$ b) $5\ m^2$
c) $0.5\ m^2$ d) $50\ m^2$

4 What is the area of this circle? (C) (1 mark)

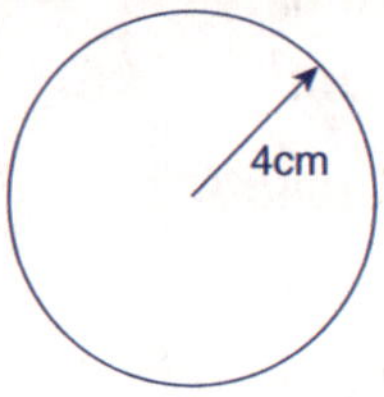

a) $25.1\ cm^2$ b) $55\ cm^2$
c) $12.6\ cm^2$ d) $50.3\ cm^2$

5 If the area of a rectangle is $20\ cm^2$ and its width is 2.5 cm, what is the length of the rectangle? (1 mark)

a) 9 cm b) 8 cm
c) 7.5 cm d) 2.5 cm

Score / 5

B Answer all parts of the questions.

1 For each of the diagrams below, decide whether the area given is true or false. (C)

a) 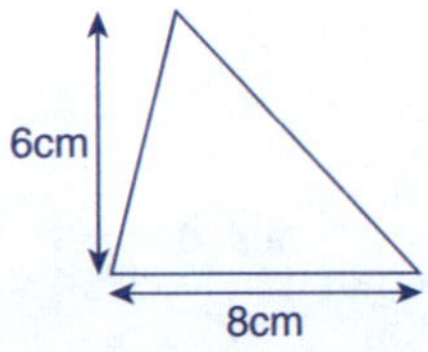

b) 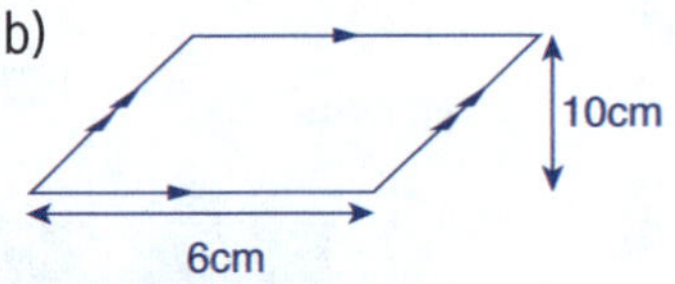

c) 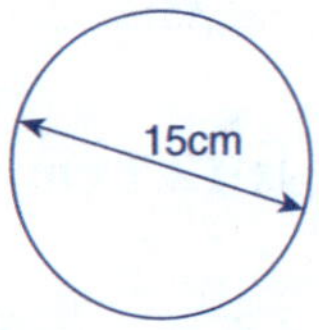

d) 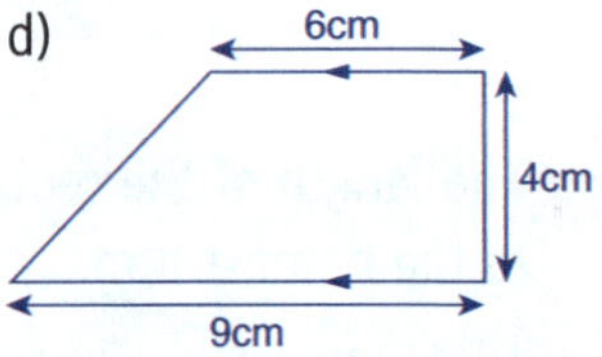

a) Area = $48\ cm^2$ .... (1 mark)
b) Area = $60\ cm^2$ .... (1 mark)
c) Area = $177\ cm^2$ .... (1 mark)
d) Area = $108\ cm^2$ .... (1 mark)

2 Calculate the perimeter of this shape. (C) (3 marks)

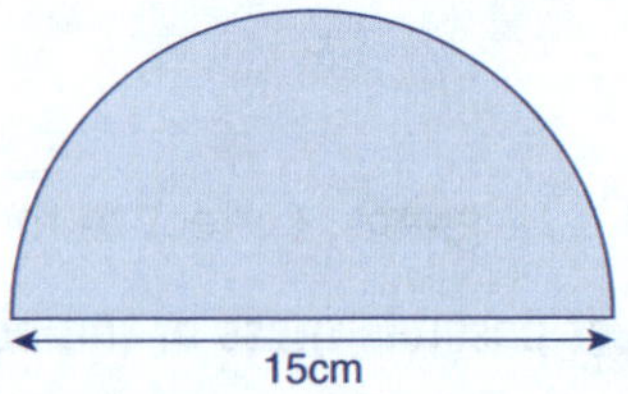

.... cm

3 Calculate the area of the shaded region in this diagram. (C) (3 marks)

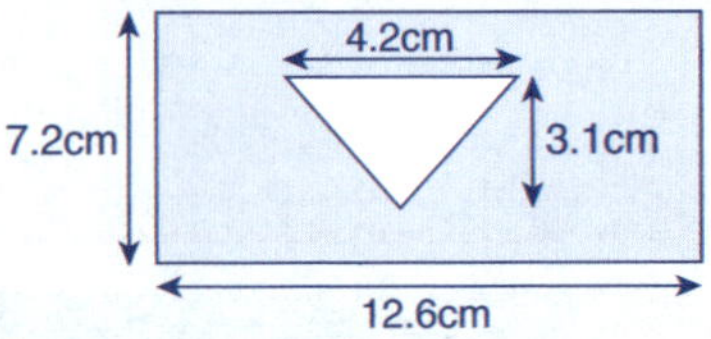

.... cm^2

Score / 10

(C) *Indicates that a calculator may be used*

C

These are GCSE-style questions. Answer all parts of the questions. Show your workings (on separate paper if necessary) and include the correct units in your answers.

1 Work out the area of the shape shown in the diagram. (C)

State the units with your answer. **(5 marks)**

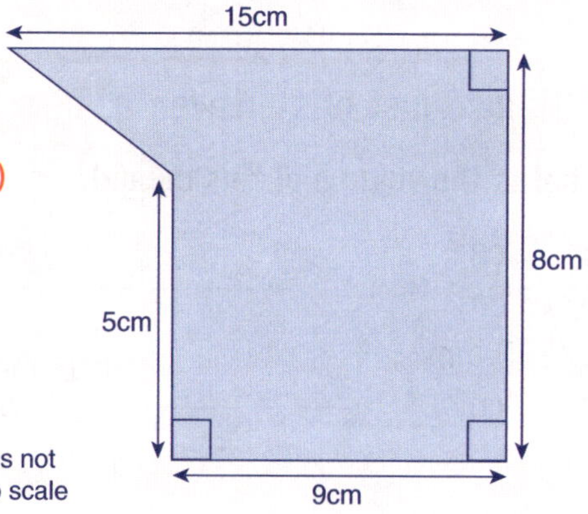

Diagrams not drawn to scale

2 Calculate the perimeter of the shape shown in the diagram. Use $\pi = 3.14$

Give your answer to 3 significant figures. (C) **(3 marks)**

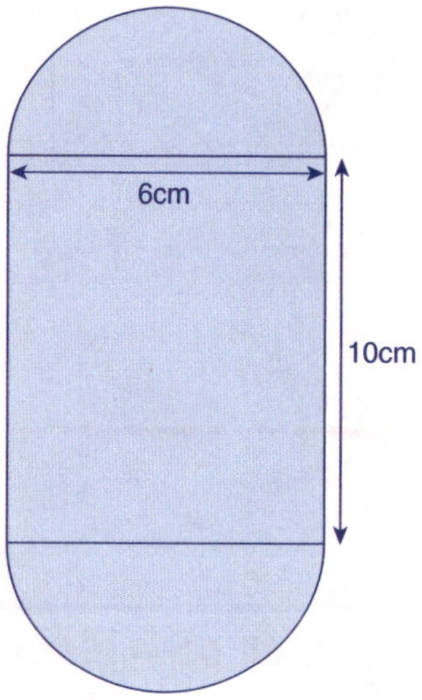

.... cm

3 The circumference of a circle is 400 cm.

Calculate the diameter of the circle.
Give your answer correct to the nearest centimetre. (C) **(3 marks)**

.... cm

4 Calculate the area of this shape.

State the units with your answer. (C) **(3 marks)**

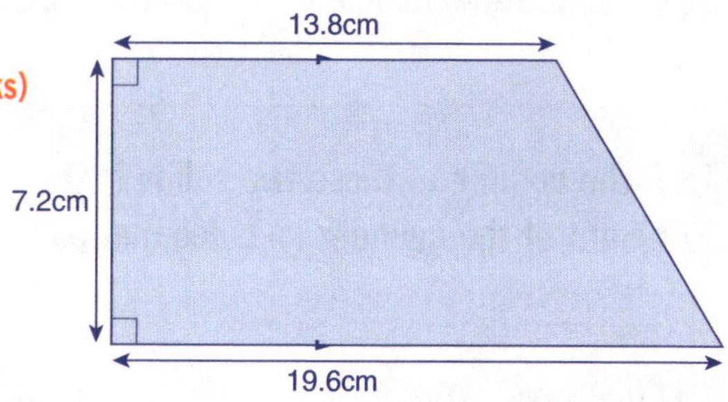

Score / 14

How well did you do? 1–8 Try again 9–14 Getting there 15–22 Good work 23–29 Excellent!

For more information on this topic see pages 70–71 of your Success Guide.

Volume of 3D shapes

A

Choose just one answer, a, b, c or d.

1 What is the volume of this cuboid? (1 mark)

a) 30 cm^3
b) 16 cm^3
c) 300 mm^3
d) 15 cm^3

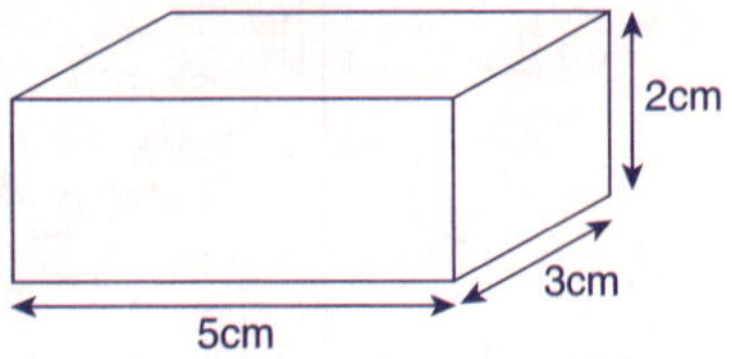

2 What is the volume of this prism? (1 mark)

a) 64 cm^3
b) 240 cm^3
c) 120 cm^3
d) 20 cm^3

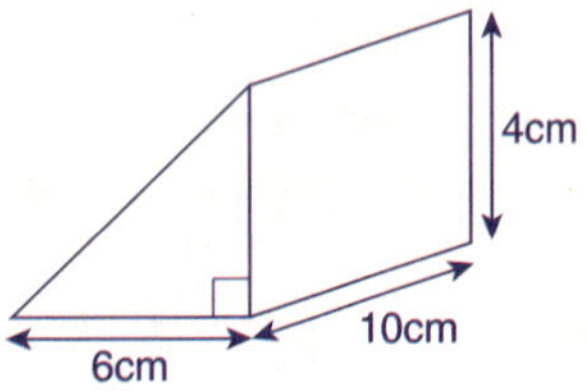

3 The volume of a cuboid is 20 cm^3. If its height is 1 cm and its width is 4 cm, what is its length? (1 mark)

a) 5 cm b) 10 cm
c) 15 cm d) 8 cm

4 A cube of volume 2 cm^3 is enlarged by a scale factor of 3. What is the volume of the enlarged cube? (1 mark)

a) 6 cm^3 b) 27 cm^3
c) 54 cm^3 d) 18 cm^3

5 If p and q represent lengths, decide what the formula $\frac{3}{5}\pi p^2 q$ shows. (1 mark)

a) circumference b) length
c) area d) volume

Score / 5

B

Answer all parts of the questions.

1 Emily says, 'The volume of this prism is 345.6 m^3.'
Decide whether Emily is correct. Show working to justify your answer. (C) (1 mark)

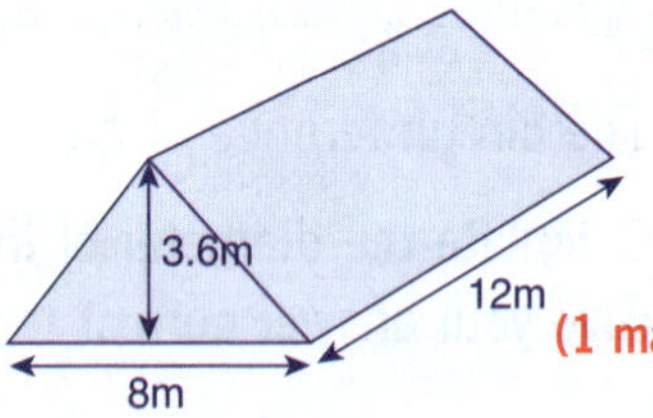

....

....

2 Calculate the volume of the cylinder, clearly stating your units. (C) (2 marks)

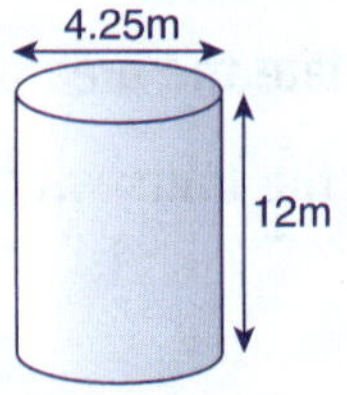

....

3 If the volume of these two solids is the same, work out the height of the cylinder to 1 decimal place. (C) (4 marks)

.... cm

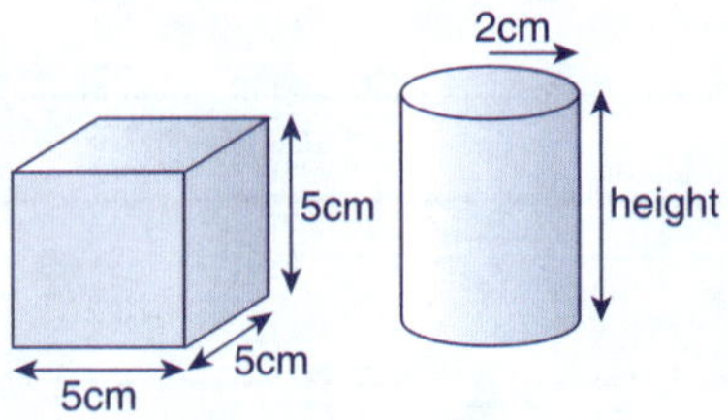

4 Lucy says, 'The volume of a sphere is given by the formula $V = 4\pi r^2$.'

Explain why she cannot be correct. (1 mark)

....

Score / 8

(C) *Indicates that a calculator may be used*

C

These are GCSE-style questions. Answer all parts of the questions. Show your workings (on separate paper if necessary) and include the correct units in your answers.

1 A cube has a surface area of 96 cm^2. Work out the volume of the cube. **(4 marks)**

.... cm

2 A door wedge is in the shape of a prism with cross section VWXY.

VW = 7 cm, VY = 15 cm, WX = 9 cm

The width of the door wedge is 8 cm.

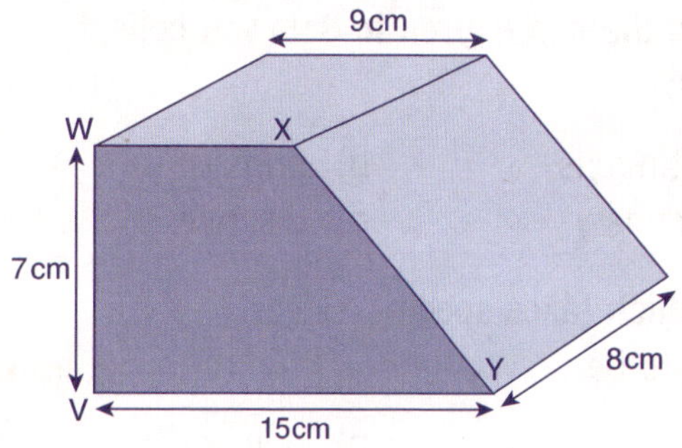

a) Calculate the volume of the door wedge. (C) **(3 marks)**

.... cm^3

b) What is the volume of the door wedge in m^3? (C) **(1 mark)**

.... m^3

3 The diagram shows a solid prism. The cross-section of the solid prism is a triangle with a base of 6 cm and a height of 8 cm. The length of the solid prism is 10 cm.

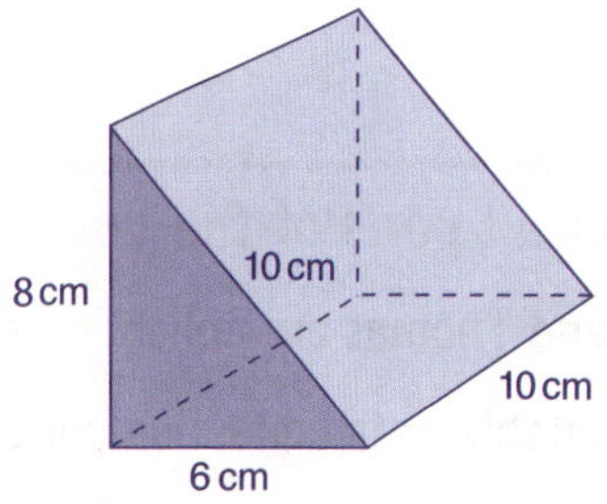

a) Work out the surface area of the solid prism. (C) **(4 marks)**

.... cm^2

b) Work out the volume of the solid prism. (C) **(2 mark)**

.... cm^3

4 Here are three expressions.

Expression	Length	Area	Volume
$4r^2p$			
$3\pi\sqrt{r^2+p^2}$			
$\frac{4\pi r^2}{3p}$			

r and p are lengths.

Put a tick in the correct column to show whether each expression can be used for length, area or volume. **(3 marks)**

5 The volume of a cube is 141 cm^3. Each length of the cube is enlarged by a scale factor of 3. What is the volume of the enlarged cube? (C) **(2 marks)**

.... cm^3

Score / 19

How well did you do? ✗ 1–7 Try again 8–15 Getting there 16–24 Good work 25–32 Excellent! ✓

For more information on this topic see pages 72–73 of your Success Guide.

Collecting data

A

Choose just one answer, a, b, c or d.

1 What is the name given to data you collect yourself? (1 mark)

a) continuous b) primary
c) secondary d) discrete

2 Data which takes specific values is said to be... (1 mark)

a) continuous b) primary
c) secondary d) discrete

3 Data which can take any value is known as... (1 mark)

a) continuous b) primary
c) secondary d) discrete

4 This type of data gives a word as an answer. (1 mark)

a) quantitative b) qualitative
c) continuous d) discrete

Score / 4

B

Answer all parts of the questions.

1 Hannah and Thomas are collecting some data on the types of books read by students.

Draw a suitable data collection sheet for this information. (3 marks)

2 Imran and Annabelle are designing a survey to use in the school. One of their questions is shown below.

How much time do you spend doing homework per night?

0–1 hrs	1–2 hrs	2–3 hrs	3–4 hrs

What is the problem with this question? Rewrite the question so that it is improved. (2 marks)

....

....

....

3 Emily decides to carry out a survey on how much football people watch on television. She decides to ask 50 men outside a football ground on Saturday afternoon. Explain why her results will be biased. (2 marks)

....

....

Score / 7

C

These are GCSE-style questions. Answer all parts of the questions. Show your workings (on separate paper if necessary) and include the correct units in your answers.

1 Amy is going to carry out a survey to record information about the colour of vehicles passing the school gate.

In the space below, draw a suitable data collection sheet that Amy could use. (3 marks)

2 Mrs Robinson is going to sell chocolate bars at the school tuck shop. She wants to know what type of chocolate bars pupils like.

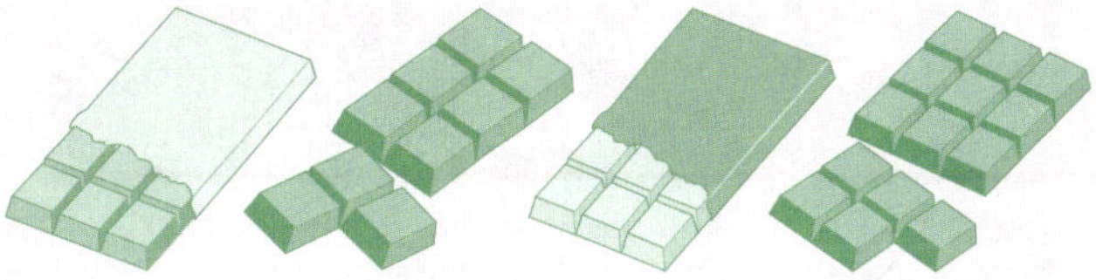

Design a suitable questionnaire she could use. (2 marks)

3 Robert is conducting a survey into television habits. One of the questions in his survey is: 'Do you watch a lot of television?'

His friend Jessica tells him that it is not a very good question.
Write down two ways in which Robert could improve the question. (2 marks)

....

....

Score /7

How well did you do? ✗ 1–4 Try again 5–8 Getting there 9–13 Good work 14–18 Excellent! ✓

For more information on this topic see pages 76–77 of your Success Guide.

Representing data

A

Choose just one answer, a, b, c or d.

For these questions, use the information shown in the frequency diagram (histogram).

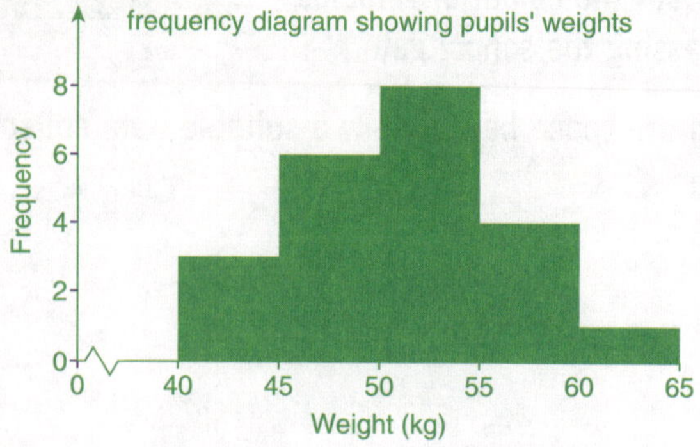

1 How many pupils had a weight between 50 and 55 kg? (1 mark)

a) 4 b) 6
c) 10 d) 8

2 How many pupils had a weight of less than 50 kg? (1 mark)

a) 7 b) 8
c) 9 d) 10

3 How many pupils had a weight of over 60 kg? (1 mark)

a) 1 b) 2
c) 3 d) 4

4 How many pupils took part in the survey? (1 mark)

a) 8 b) 22
c) 5 d) 20

Score / 4

B

Answer all parts of the questions.

1 Sarah carried out a survey to find the favourite flavours of crisps of students in her class. Her results are shown in the table below. (C)

Crisp flavour	Number of students
Cheese and Onion	7
Salt and Vinegar	10
Beef	6
Smokey Bacon	1

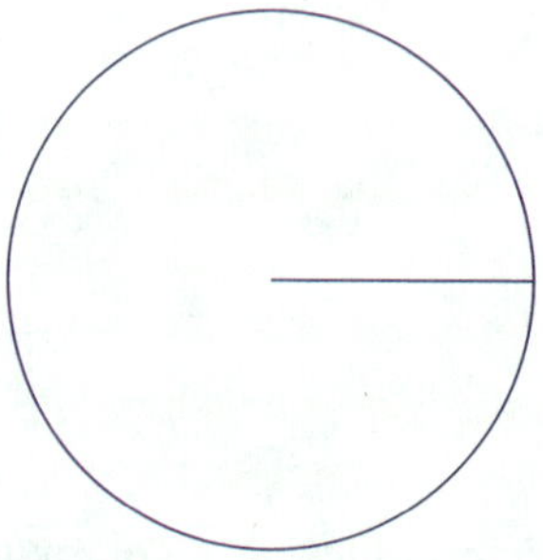

Draw an accurate pie chart to show this information. (4 marks)

2 The number of hours of sunshine during the first seven days in May are shown on the line graph. Use the information on the graph to complete the table. (3 marks)

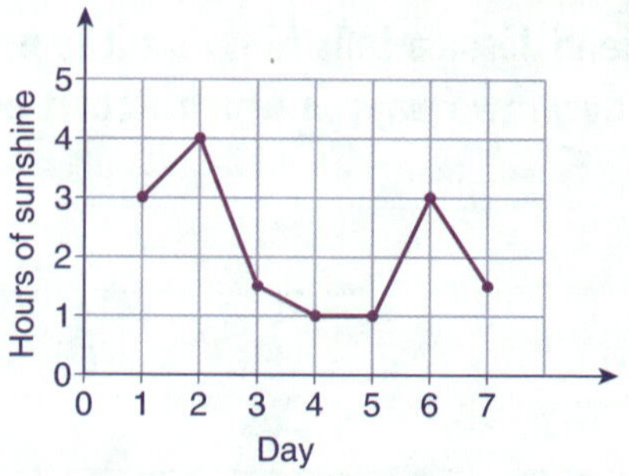

Day	1	2	3	4	5	6	7
Hrs of sunshine	3		1.5	1	1		

Score / 7

(C) *Indicates that a calculator may be used*

C

These are GCSE-style questions. Answer all parts of the questions. Show your workings (on separate paper if necessary) and include the correct units in your answers.

1 The pictogram shows the number of DVDs borrowed from a shop on a Friday and Saturday.

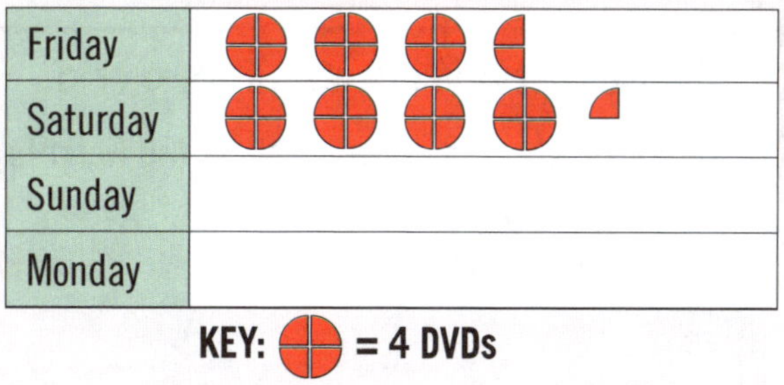

a) Write down the number of DVDs borrowed on

i) Friday ....

ii) Saturday. .... (2 marks)

b) On Sunday, 13 DVDs were borrowed. On Monday, 6 DVDs were borrowed.

Show this information on the pictogram. (2 marks)

2 A vending machine is emptied every day. The pie chart represents the number of each type of coin in the machine.

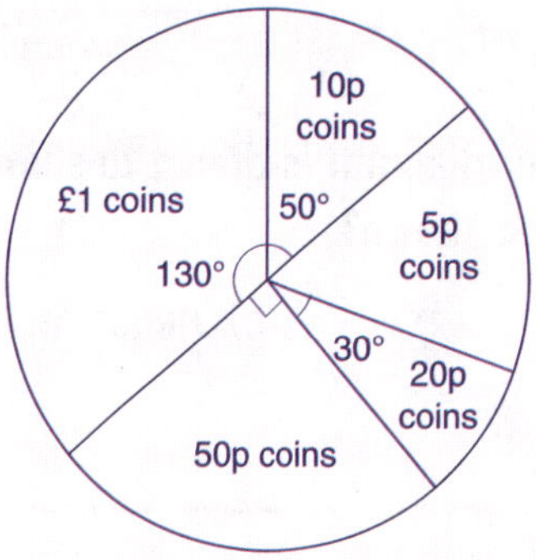

The machine contains 150 ten-pence coins.

a) How many one-pound coins are there? (C) (1 mark)

....

b) Calculate the total amount of money in the machine. (C) (4 marks)

....

....

3 The table shows the heights of a class of children.

Height in cm	Frequency
$130 \le h < 135$	5
$135 \le h < 140$	9
$140 \le h < 145$	7
$145 \le h < 150$	4
$150 \le h < 155$	5
$155 \le h < 160$	2

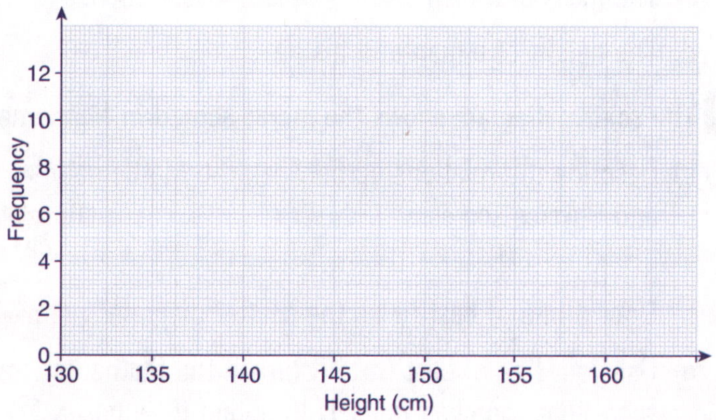

Draw a frequency polygon for this data on the grid provided. (3 marks)

Score / 12

How well did you do? 1–4 Try again 5–9 Getting there 10–16 Good work 17–23 Excellent!

Scatter diagrams and correlation

A Choose just one answer, a, b, c or d.

1 **A scatter diagram is drawn to show the heights and weights of some students. What type of correlation is shown?** (1 mark)

a) zero
b) negative
c) positive
d) scattered

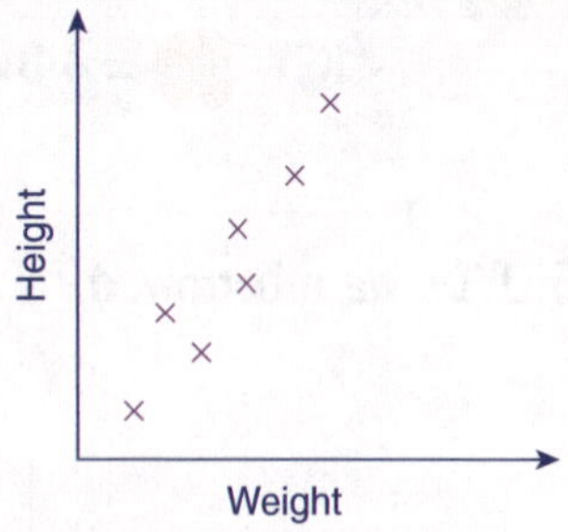

2 **A scatter diagram is drawn to show the maths scores and the heights of a group of students. What type of correlation is shown?** (1 mark)

a) zero
b) negative
c) positive
d) scattered

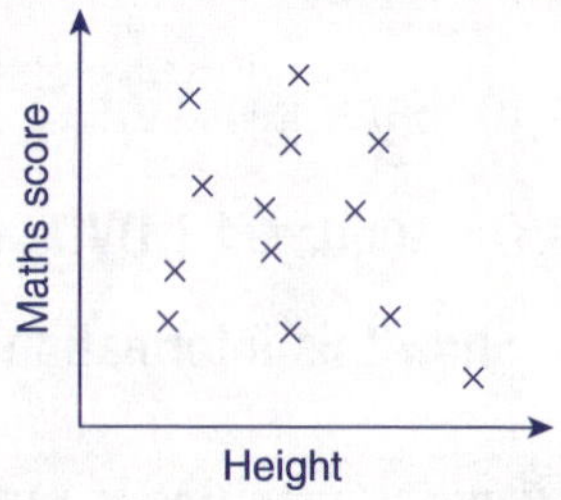

3 **A scatter diagram is drawn to show the age of some cars and their value. What type of correlation would be shown?** (1 mark)

a) zero b) negative c) positive d) scattered

Score /3

B Answer all parts of the questions.

1 **Some statements have been written on cards.**

Positive Correlation	Negative Correlation	No Correlation

Decide which card best describes these relationships.

a) The temperature and sales of ice lollies .... (1 mark)
b) The temperature and sales of woollen gloves .... (1 mark)
c) The mass of a man and his waist measurement .... (1 mark)
d) The height of a man and his IQ .... (1 mark)

2 **The scatter diagram shows the marks scored in Mathematics and Physics examinations.**

a) Describe the relationship between the Mathematics and Physics scores. (1 mark)

....

b) Draw a line of best fit on the scatter diagram. (1 mark)

c) Use your line of best fit to estimate the Mathematics score that Jonathan is likely to obtain if he has a Physics score of 75%. (1 mark)

....

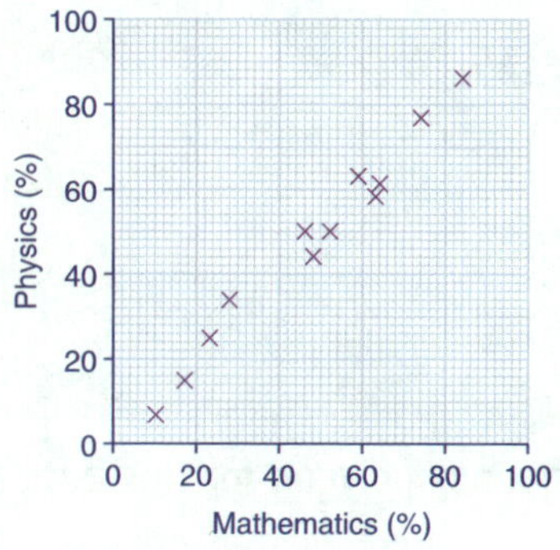

Score /7

C

These are GCSE-style questions. Answer all parts of the questions. Show your workings (on separate paper if necessary) and include the correct units in your answers.

1 **The table shows the ages of some children and the total number of hours sleep they had between noon on Saturday and noon on Sunday.**

Age (years)	2	6	5	3	12	9	2	10	5	10	7	11	12	3
No. of hours' sleep	15	13.1	13.2	14.8	10.1	11.8	15.6	11.6	13.5	11.8	12.8	10.2	9.5	14

a) Plot the information from the table as a scatter diagram. (4 marks)

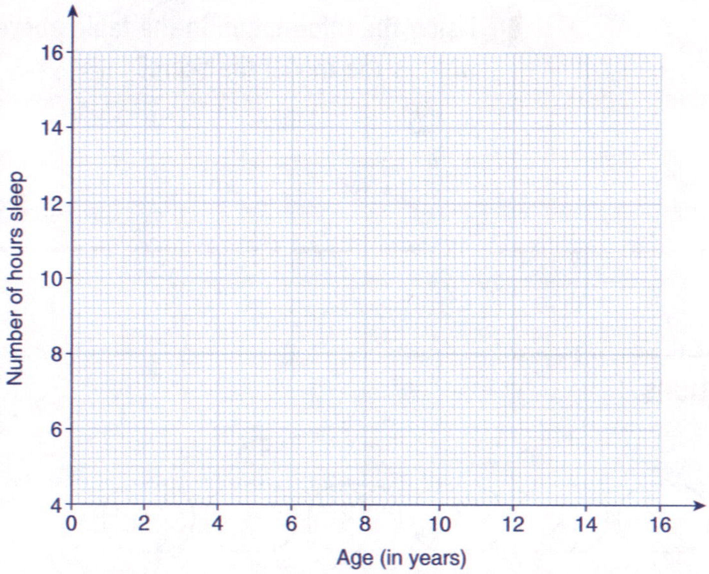

b) Describe the correlation between the age of the children in years and the number of hours sleep they had. (2 marks)

....

....

c) Draw a line of best fit on your scatter diagram. (1 mark)

d) Estimate the total number of hours sleep for a 4-year-old child. (2 marks)

....

e) Explain why the line of best fit only gives an estimate for the number of hours slept. (2 marks)

....

....

Score / 11

How well did you do? ✗ 1–5 Try again 6–11 Getting there 12–16 Good work 17–21 Excellent! ✓

For more information on this topic see pages 80–81 of your Success Guide.

Averages 1

A Choose just one answer, a, b, c or d.

1 **What is the mean of this set of data?**
2, 7, 1, 4, 2, 6, 2, 5, 2, 6 (1 mark)

a) 4.2 b) 3.6
c) 3.7 d) 3.9

2 **What is the median value of the set of data used in question 1?** (1 mark)

a) 2 b) 3
c) 4 d) 5

3 **What is the range of this set of data?**
2, 7, 1, 4, 11, 9, 6 (1 mark)

a) 1 b) 6
c) 11 d) 10

4 **A dice is thrown and the scores are noted. The results are shown in the table below. What is the mean die score?** (C) (1 mark)

Die score	1	2	3	4	5	6
Frequency	12	15	10	8	14	13

a) 5 b) 3
c) 4 d) 3.5

5 **Using the information in the table above, what is the modal die score?** (1 mark)

a) 15 b) 2
c) 4 d) 8

Score / 5

B Answer all parts of the questions.

1 **Here are some number cards.**

8 7 11 4 2 1 3 12 4 4

Decide whether the following statements, which refer to the number cards above, are true or false.

a) The range of the number cards is 1–11. .... (1 mark)

b) The mean of the number cards is 5.6. .... (1 mark)

c) The median of the number cards is 5. .... (1 mark)

d) The mode of the number cards is 4. .... (1 mark)

2 **A baked beans factory claims that 'On average, a tin of baked beans contains 141 beans.'**
In order to check the accuracy of this claim, a sample of 20 tins was taken and the number of beans in each tin counted. The results are shown in the table below. (C)

Number of beans	137	138	139	140	141	142	143	144
Number of tins	1	1	1	2	5	4	4	2

a) Calculate the mean number of beans per tin. .... (1 mark)

b) Explain briefly whether you think the manufacturer is justified in making its claim. (C) (1 mark)

....

3 **The mean of 7, 9, 10, 18, x and 17 is 13. What is the value of x?** .... (C) (2 marks)

Score / 8

(C) *Indicates that a calculator may be used*

C

These are GCSE-style questions. Answer all parts of the questions. Show your workings (on separate paper if necessary) and include the correct units in your answers.

1 Grace made a list of the ages of some children in her swimming club.

7, 8, 7, 14, 10, 12, 12, 7, 12, 12, 11, 15

a) Find the median age of the children. (2 marks)

....

b) Find the range of the ages of the children. (1 mark)

....

c) Find the mean age of the children. (C) (3 marks)

....

....

2 Some students took a test. The table gives information about their marks in the test.

Mark	Frequency
3	2
4	5
5	11
6	2

Work out the mean mark. (C) (3 marks)

....

....

3 Simon has sat three examinations. His mean score is 65. To pass the unit, he needs to get an average of 69.

What score must he get in the final examination to pass the unit? (C) (3 marks)

....

....

4 A company employs 3 women and 7 men.

The mean weekly wage of the 10 employees is £464.

The mean weekly wage of the 3 women is £520.

Calculate the mean weekly wage of the 7 men. (C) (4 marks)

....

....

Score / 16

How well did you do? ✗ 1–6 Try again 7–12 Getting there 13–22 Good work 23–29 Excellent! ✓

For more information on this topic see pages 82–83 of your Success Guide.

Averages 2

A Choose just one answer, a, b, c or d.

The following questions are based on the information given in the table below about the time taken in seconds to swim 50 metres.

Time (t seconds)	Frequency (f)
$0 \le t < 30$	1
$30 \le t < 60$	2
$60 \le t < 90$	4
$90 \le t < 120$	6
$120 \le t < 150$	7
$150 \le t < 180$	2

1 How many people swam 50 metres in less than 60 seconds? (1 mark)

a) 2 b) 4
c) 3 d) 6

2 Which of the intervals is the modal class? (1 mark)

a) $60 \le t < 90$ b) $120 \le t < 150$
c) $30 \le t < 60$ d) $90 \le t < 120$

3 Which of the class intervals contains the median value? (1 mark)

a) $90 \le t < 120$ b) $150 \le t < 180$
c) $120 \le t < 150$ d) $60 \le t < 90$

4 Which of these is an estimate for the mean time to swim 50 metres? (C) (1 mark)

a) 105 seconds b) 385 seconds
c) 100 seconds d) 125 seconds

Score /4

B Answer all parts of the questions.

1 The length of some seedlings are shown in the table below.

Length (mm)	Number of seedlings
$0 \le L < 10$	3
$10 \le L < 20$	5
$20 \le L < 30$	9
$30 \le L < 40$	2
$40 \le L < 50$	1

Calculate an estimate for the mean length of the seedlings. (C) (4 marks)

Mean = ... mm

2 The stem-and-leaf diagram shows the marks gained by some students in a Mathematics examination.

Stem	Leaf
1	2 5 7
2	6 9
3	4 5 5 7
4	2 7 7 7 7
5	2

Stem = 10 marks
Key: 1 | 2 = 12 marks

Using the stem-and-leaf diagram, calculate:

a) the mode .... (1 mark)

b) the median .... (1 mark)

c) the range .... (1 mark)

Score /7

(C) *Indicates that a calculator may be used*

C

These are GCSE-style questions. Answer all parts of the questions. Show your workings (on separate paper if necessary) and include the correct units in your answers.

1 A psychologist records the time, to the nearest minute, taken by 20 students to complete a logic problem.
Here are her results.

12	22	31	36	35	14	27	23	19	25
15	17	15	27	32	38	41	18	27	18

Draw a stem-and-leaf diagram to show this information. (4 marks)

2 John asks 100 people how much they spent last year on newspapers.
His results are in the table below.

Amount £ (x)	Frequency
$0 \leq x < 10$	12
$10 \leq x < 20$	20
$20 \leq x < 30$	15
$30 \leq x < 40$	18
$40 \leq x < 50$	14
$50 \leq x < 60$	18
$60 \leq x < 70$	3

a) Calculate an estimate of the mean amount spent on newspapers. (C) (4 marks)

....

b) Explain briefly why this value of the mean is only an estimate. (1 mark)

....

c) Calculate the class interval in which the median lies. (2 marks)

....

Score /11

How well did you do? ✗ 1–6 Try again 7–11 Getting there 12–16 Good work 17–22 Excellent! ✓

For more information on this topic see pages 84–85 of your Success Guide.

Probability 1

A

Choose just one answer, a, b, c or d.

1 A bag of sweets contains 5 hard centres and 3 soft centres. What is the probability of choosing a hard centre if the sweet is drawn out of the bag at random? (1 mark)

a) $\frac{3}{5}$ b) $\frac{3}{8}$ c) $\frac{5}{8}$ d) $\frac{1}{2}$

2 The probability that Highbury football club win a football match is $\frac{12}{17}$. What is the probability that they do not win the football match? (1 mark)

a) $\frac{5}{12}$ b) $\frac{17}{29}$ c) $\frac{12}{17}$ d) $\frac{5}{17}$

3 A fair die is thrown 600 times. On how many of these throws would you expect to get a 4? (1 mark)

a) 40 b) 600 c) 100 d) 580

4 A fair dice is thrown 500 times. If a 6 comes up 87 times, what is the relative frequency? (1 mark)

a) $\frac{1}{6}$ b) $\frac{87}{500}$ c) $\frac{10}{600}$ d) $\frac{1}{587}$

5 The probability that it will rain tomorrow is 0.35. What is the probability that it will not rain tomorrow? (1 mark)

a) 0.65 b) 0.35 c) 0.25 d) 1.35

Score / 5

B

Answer all parts of the questions.

1 The letters M A T H E M A T I C S are each placed on a separate piece of card and put into a bag. Stuart picks out a card at random.
What is the probability he picks the following cards? (4 marks)

a) The letter T ....
b) The letter M ....
c) The letters A or C ....
d) The letter R ....

2 The probability that Robert wins a tennis match is 0.6.
What is the probability that Robert does not win the tennis match? .... (1 mark)

3 Decide whether each of these statements is true or false.

a) The probability of getting a six when a fair die is thrown is $\frac{1}{6}$. .... (1 mark)

b) The probability of passing a test in physics is 0.3. If 100 students sit the test, the number expected to pass would be 3. .... (1 mark)

c) The probability that Conkers football team win a match is 0.8.
The probability that they will not win the game is 0.4. .... (1 mark)

4 The probability of achieving a grade A in French is 0.2.
If 500 students sit the exam, how many would you expect to achieve a grade A? .... (2 marks)

Score / 10

C

These are GCSE-style questions. Answer all parts of the questions. Show your workings (on separate paper if necessary) and include the correct units in your answers.

1 A bag contains 4 blue, 2 green and 6 red counters. A counter is chosen at random from the bag.

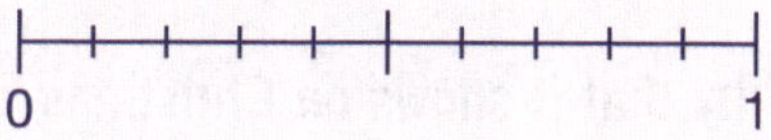

On the probability scale above:

a) label with the letter R the probability of choosing a red counter. (1 mark)
b) label with the letter B the probability of choosing a blue counter. (1 mark)
c) label with the letter W the probability of choosing a white counter. (1 mark)
d) label with the letter P the probability of choosing a blue, green or red counter. (1 mark)

2 There are 20 different coloured sweets in a jar. The colour of each sweet can be red, green, yellow or blue. The table shows how many sweets of each colour are in the jar.

Colour	Red	Green	Yellow	Blue
Number	4	5	7	4

Reece picks one sweet at random from the jar.

a) Write down the probability that he will pick:

i) a green sweet .... (1 mark)

ii) a yellow sweet .... (1 mark)

b) Write down the probability that he will not pick a blue sweet. .... (2 marks)

3 A bag contains different beads of four different colours – red, white, blue and pink.

The table shows the probability of taking a bead of a particular colour at random.

Colour	Red	White	Blue	Pink
Probability	0.25	0.1		0.3

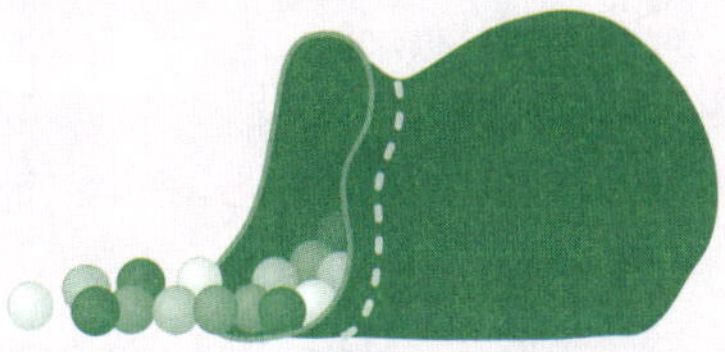

Jackie is going to take a bead at random and then put it back in the bag.

a) i) Work out the probability that Jackie will take out a blue bead. .... (2 marks)

ii) Write down the probability that Jackie will take out a black bead. .... (1 mark)

b) Jackie will take out a bead from the bag at random 200 times, replacing the bead each time. Work out an estimate for the number of times that Jackie will take a red bead. (2 marks)

....

Score / 13

How well did you do? 1–6 Try again 7–13 Getting there 14–21 Good work 22–28 Excellent!

For more information on this topic see pages 86–89 of your Success Guide.

Probability 2

A Choose just one answer, a, b, c or d.

1 **Two dice are thrown and their scores are added. What is the probability of a score of 5?** (1 mark)

a) $\frac{1}{2}$ b) $\frac{2}{12}$ c) $\frac{4}{36}$ d) $\frac{5}{36}$

2 **Two dice are thrown and their scores are multiplied. What is the probability of a score of 1?** (1 mark)

a) $\frac{1}{36}$ b) $\frac{1}{12}$ c) $\frac{2}{12}$ d) $\frac{2}{36}$

3 **The probability that it snows on Christmas Day is 0.2. What is the probability that it will not snow on Christmas Day?** (1 mark)

a) 0.8 b) 0.4 c) 0.16 d) 0.04

4 **The probability that Fiona is in the hockey team is 0.7. What is the probability that Fiona is not in the hockey team?** (1 mark)

a) 1.7 b) 9.3 c) 0.7 d) 0.3

Score / 4

B Answer all parts of the questions.

1 **Two spinners are spun at the same time and their scores are added.**

Spinner 1

Spinner 2
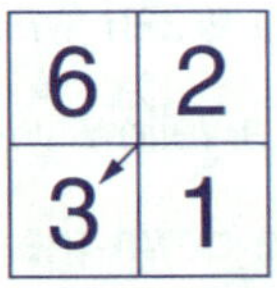

a) Complete the sample space diagram to show the possible outcomes. (2 marks)

Spinner 1 (across), Spinner 2 (down)

	1	2	3	3
1	2			
2			5	
3		5		
6		8	9	

b) Find the probability of:

i) a score of 4 .... (1 mark)

ii) a score of 9 .... (1 mark)

iii) a score of 1 .... (1 mark)

2 **For lunch Charlotte has a sandwich and a drink. For her sandwich she can choose ham or cheese or beef. For her drink she can choose orange juice or tea. List all the possible lunches that Charlotte can have.** (2 marks)

....

....

3 **The probability that Michelle finishes first in a swimming race is 0.3. What is the probability that Michelle does not finish first?** .... (2 marks)

Score / 9

C

These are GCSE-style questions. Answer all parts of the questions. Show your workings (on separate paper if necessary) and include the correct units in your answers.

1 Two fair dice are thrown together and their scores are added.

a) Work out the probability of a score of 7. .... (2 marks)

b) Work out the probability of a score of 9. .... (2 marks)

2 A youth club has 75 members. The table below shows some information about the members.

	Under 13 years old	13 years and over	Total
Boys	15		42
Girls		21	
Total			75

a) Complete the table. (3 marks)

b) One of the club members is picked at random.

Write down the probability that this member is under 13 years old. .... (1 mark)

3 Some students are given a choice of activities. In the morning they can do swimming (S), tennis (T) or Art (A), and in the afternoon they have a choice of football (F) or swimming.
Write down all the possible combinations that the students can choose if they do one activity in the morning and one activity in the afternoon. (2 marks)

....

....

....

Score / 10

How well did you do? 1–5 Try again 6–11 Getting there 12–18 Good work 19–23 Excellent!

For more information on this topic see pages 86–89 of your Success Guide.

Mixed GCSE-style Questions

Answer these questions. Show full working out.

1 a) Write the number sixteen thousand, four hundred and sixty-two in figures. **(1 mark)**

....

b) Write down the value of the 3 in the number 743 271. **(1 mark)**

....

c) Write the number 7942 rounded to the nearest ten. **(1 mark)**

....

2 Look at the shaded shape on the centimetre grid.

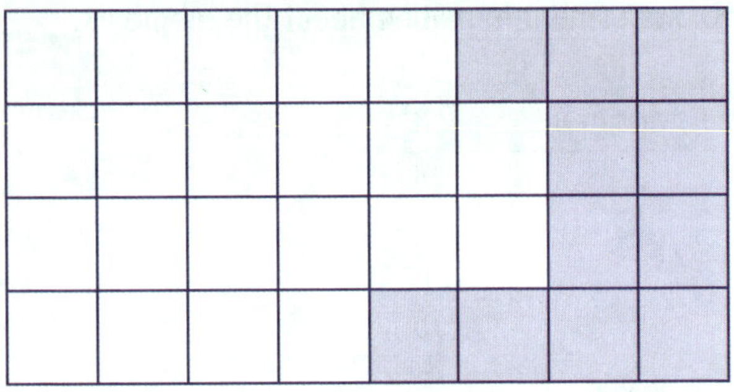

a) i) Find the area of the shaded shape. **(2 marks)**

.... cm^2

ii) Find the perimeter of the shaded shape.

.... cm

b) The diagram shows a square.
Draw the lines of symmetry on the square. **(2 marks)**

3 a) **Complete the table by writing a sensible metric unit on each dotted line. The first one has been done for you.**

The distance from Manchester to London	226 kilometres
The volume of tea in a mug	305 ....
The weight of a £1 coin	11 ....
The height of a room	325 ....

b) **Change 6300 grams into kilograms.** (1 mark)

.... kg

c) **Change 5 inches into centimetres.** (1 mark)

.... cm

4 Here is a list of 8 numbers.

2, 7, 15, 18, 27, 39, 45, 46

a) **Write down two numbers from the list with a sum of 63.** (1 mark)

....

b) **Write down a number from the list which is a factor of 21.** (1 mark)

....

c) **Write down a number from the list which is a cube number.** (1 mark)

....

d) **Write down a number from the list which is a multiple of 5.** (1 mark)

....

5 **Work out 279 × 48.** (3 marks)

....

6 **On the grid, enlarge the shape with a scale factor of 2.** (2 marks)

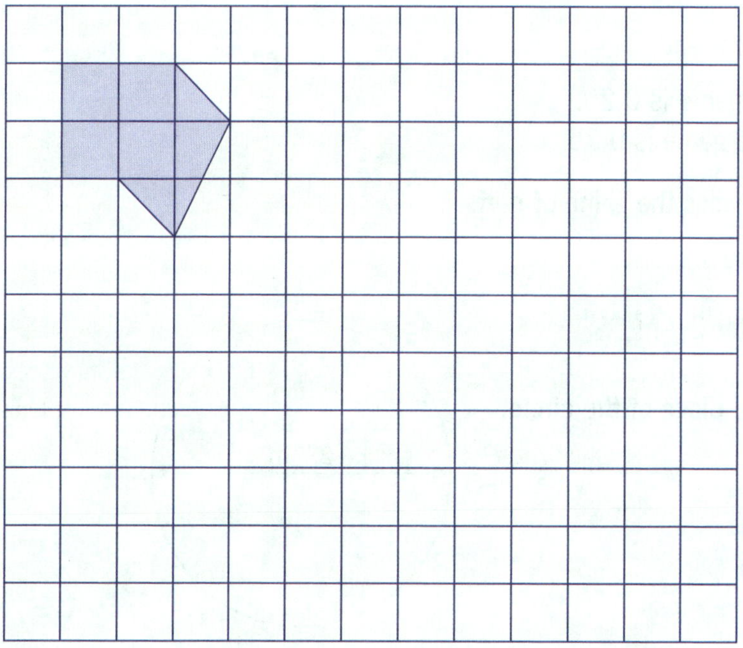

7 a) **Simplify $3a + 5b + 2a - 4b$** (2 marks)

....

b) **Simplify $7x - 2y + 3x - 5y$** (2 marks)

....

c) **Simplify $5a^2 - 3a^2$** (1 mark)

....

8 In the diagram, WXY is a straight line.

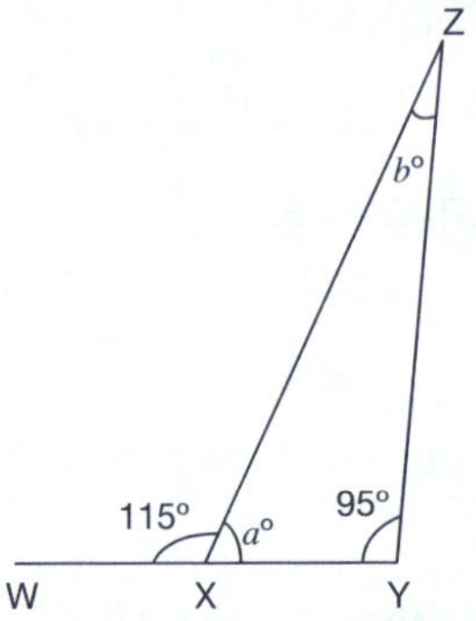

a) i) **Work out the size of the angle marked a.** (2 marks)

.... °

ii) **Give a reason for your answer.**

....

b) i) **Work out the size of the angle marked b.** (2 marks)

.... °

ii) **Give a reason for your answer.**

....

9 **Write the ratio 32 : 8 in its simplest form.** (1 mark)

....

10 A game of darts can be won, or drawn or lost.
Ahmed plays a game of darts with his friend.

The probability that Ahmed wins the game is 0.25.
The probability that Ahmed draws the game is 0.35.

Work out the probability that Ahmed loses the game of darts. (2 marks)

....

11 The diagram shows a circle of diameter 2.7 m
Work out the area of the circle. (C)
Give your answer correct to 1 decimal place of the circle. (3 marks)

.... m^2

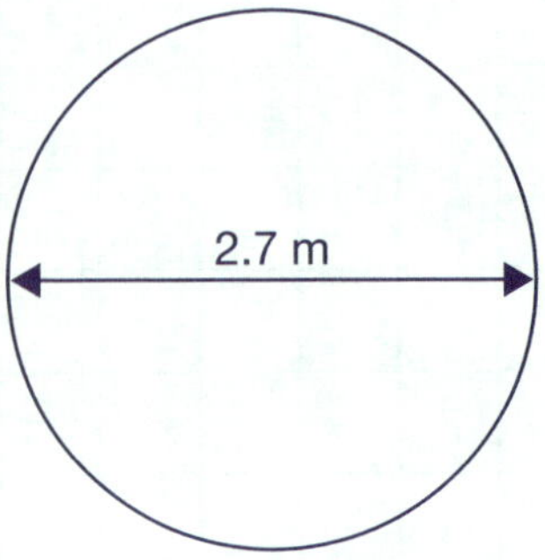

(C) *Indicates that a calculator may be used*

12 The table gives information about the brands of television available in a shop.

Brand of television	Number in stock
Sharp	6
Panasonic	10
Toshiba	2

(C)

Draw an accurate pie chart to show this information. (C) **(3 marks)**

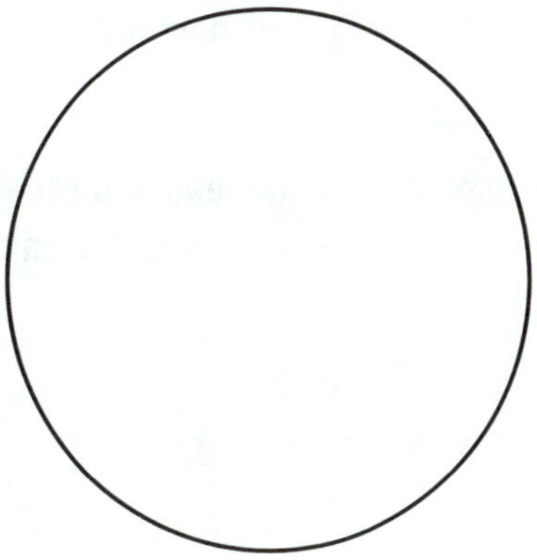

13 Katy sells CDs.
She sells each CD for £9.20 plus VAT at 17.5%.
She sells 127 CDs.
Work out how much money Katy receives. (C) **(4 marks)**

£..

14 Here is a diagram showing the side views of a model.

The cubes are either pink or white.

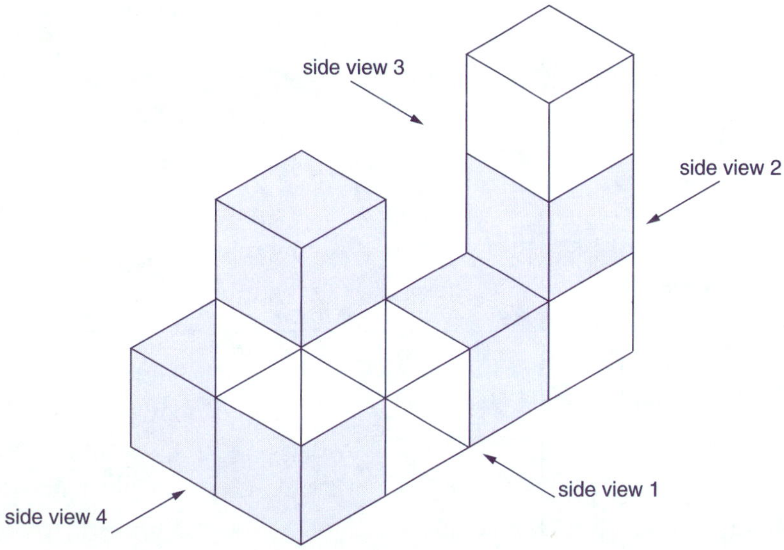

These drawings show the side views of the model. Write the numbers to show which side view each drawing represents. **(2 marks)**

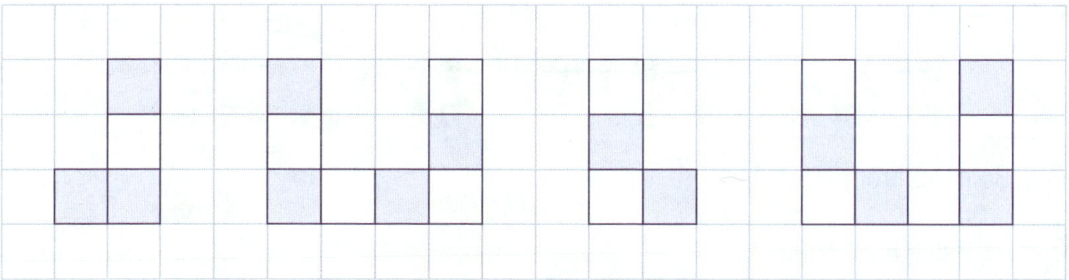

a) side view .... **b) side view** .... **c) side view** .... **d) side view** ....

(C) *Indicates that a calculator may be used*

15 **Work these out.**

a) 4.23 × 6.1 .... **(2 marks)**

b) 10.53 ÷ 3.9 .... **(2 marks)**

c) Estimate the value of $\frac{8.9 \times 5.2}{10.1}$ .... **(2 marks)**

16 The cost of 8 pencils is £1.92.

a) Work out the cost of 14 pencils. **(2 marks)**

£ ....

b) The probability that the lead will break on first use is 0.12. Work out the probability that the lead of a pencil picked at random will not break. **(1 mark)**

....

17 Here are the first four terms of an arithmetic sequence.

5, 9, 13, 17

Find an expression, in terms of n, for the nth term of the sequence. **(2 marks)**

....

18 **Draw the graph of $y = 4 - 3x$ on the grid below.** **(3 marks)**

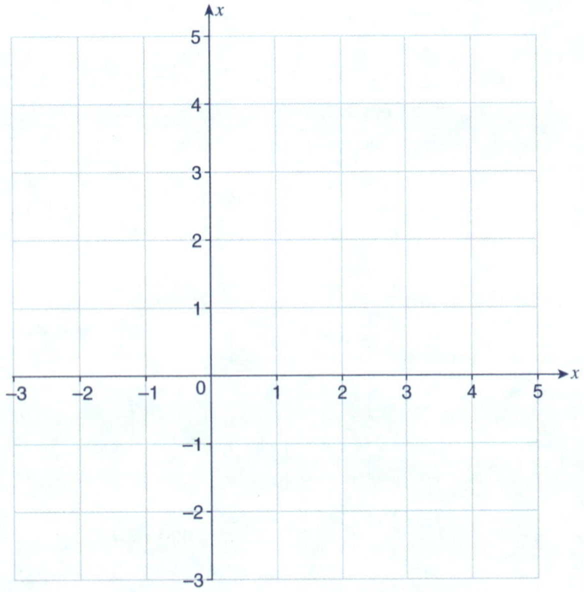

19 The diagram shows the positions of three towns, A, B and C. Town C is due east of towns A and B. Town B is due east of A.

Town B is $3\frac{1}{3}$ miles from town A.

Town C is $1\frac{1}{4}$ miles from town B.

Calculate the number of miles between town A and town C. **(3 marks)**

.... miles

20 Here are the ages in years of the members of a golf club.

9	42	37	28	36	44	47	43	62	19	17	36	40
56	58	32	18	41	52	42	54	38	27	29	32	51

In the space provided, draw a stem and leaf diagram to show these ages. (3 marks)

21 The diagram shows a shape, made from a semicircle, a rectangle and a triangle.

The diameter of the semicircle is 4 cm.

The length of the rectangle is 7 cm.

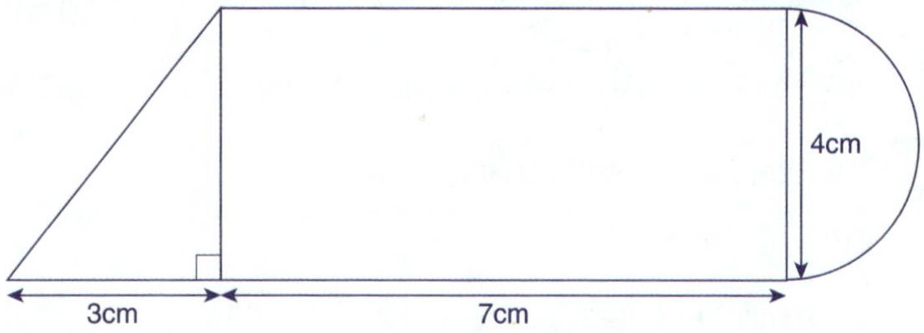

Calculate the perimeter of the shape.

Give your answer correct to 3 significant figures. (5 marks)

.... cm

22 $2.4 \times 320 = 768$

Use this result to write down the answers to these.

a) 2.4×32 .... (1 mark)

b) 2.4×3.2 .... (1 mark)

c) 0.24×0.32 .... (1 mark)

23 **a) Solve $5n + 2 = 12$** $n =$ .... (2 marks)

b) Solve $4a + 3 = 2a + 8$ $a =$ .... (2 marks)

c) Solve $5x - 2 = 3(x + 6)$ $x =$ .... (2 marks)

d) Solve $\frac{3-2x}{4} = 2$ $x =$ .... (2 marks)

e) Simplify these.

i) $p^4 \times p^6$ .... (1 mark)

ii) $\frac{p^7}{p^3}$ .... (1 mark)

iii) $\frac{p^4 \times p^5}{p}$ .... (1 mark)

24 Megan bought a TV for £700. Each year, the TV depreciated by 20%.

Work out the value of the TV two years after she bought it. Ⓒ £.. **(3 marks)**

25 The table gives the times to the nearest minute taken to complete a puzzle.

Time (nearest min)	Frequency
$0 \le t < 10$	5
$10 \le t < 20$	12
$20 \le t < 30$	8
$30 \le t < 40$	5

Calculate an estimate for the mean number of minutes taken to complete the puzzle. Ⓒ **(4 marks)**

Mean .... minutes

26 The diagram shows a triangle ABC.

AB = 6.2 cm, BC = 4.9 cm

Work out the length x of the side AC. Ⓒ
Give your answer to 1 decimal place.

....

.... cm

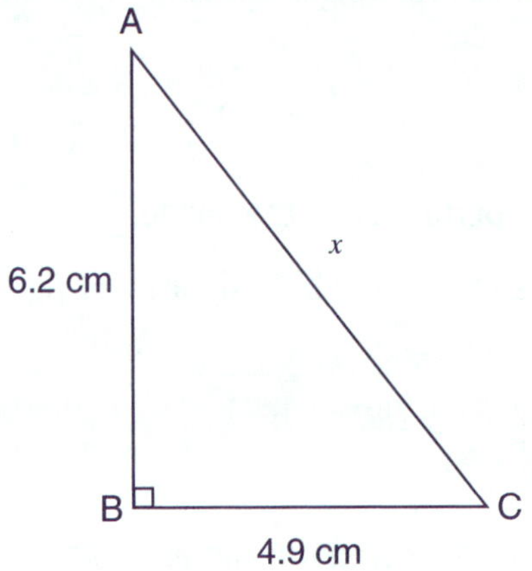

(3 marks)

Ⓒ *Indicates that a calculator may be used*

Answers to mixed questions

1 a) 16 462
b) 3 thousands
c) 7940

2 a) i) 11 cm^2
ii) 18 cm
b)

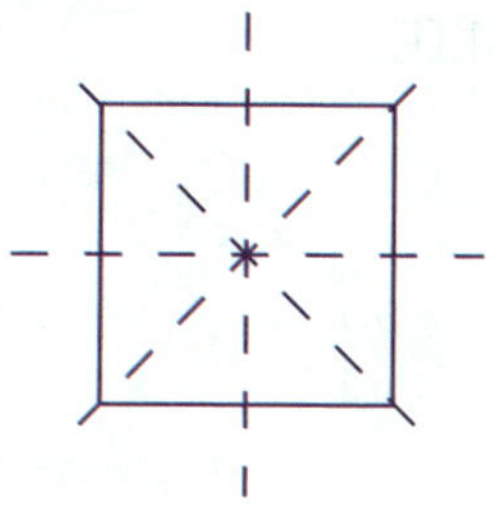

3 a) 305 ml
11 g
325 cm
b) 6.3 kg
c) 12.5 cm

4 a) 45 and 18
b) 7
c) 27
d) 15 or 45

5 13 392

6

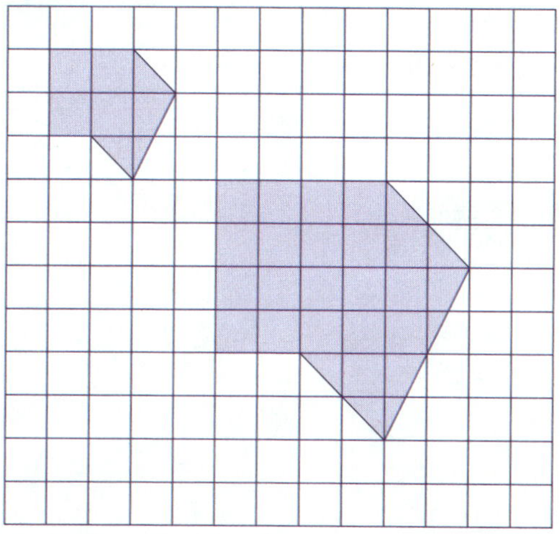

7 a) $5a + b$
b) $10x - 7y$
c) $2a^2$

8 a) i) 65°
ii) Angles on a straight line add up to 180°.
b) i) 20°
ii) Angles in a triangle add up to 180°.
(95° + 65° + 20° = 180°)

9 4 : 1

10 1 − (0.25 + 0.35)
= 1 − 0.6
= 0.4

11 Area = $\pi \times r^2$ $r = \frac{2.7}{2}$ $r = 1.35$
Area = $\pi \times 1.35^2$
= 5.725
= 5.7 cm^2 (to 1 d.p.)

12

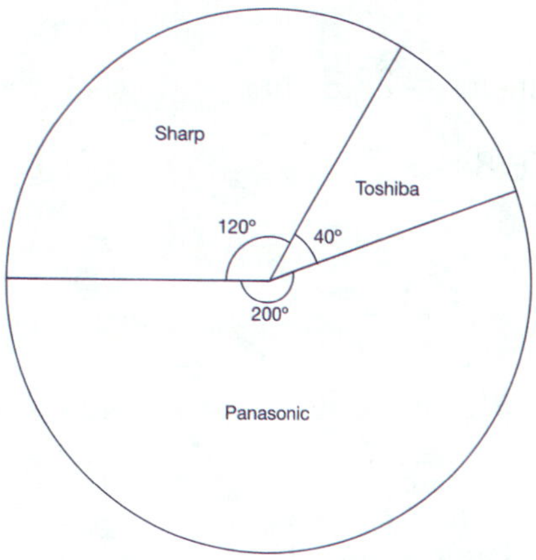

13 9.20 × 1.175 = £10.81 with VAT
for each CD
127 × £10.81
= £1372.87

14 a) side view 4
b) side view 1
c) side view 2
d) side view 3

15 a) 25.803 b) 2.7 c) 4.5

16 a) £3.36 b) 0.88

17 $4n + 1$

18

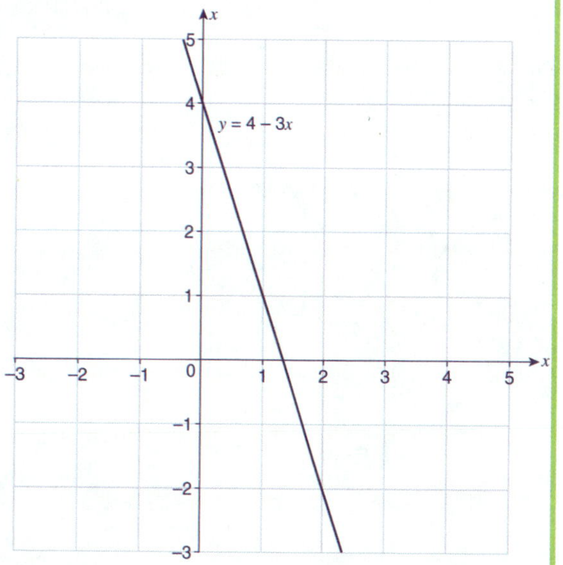

19 $4\frac{7}{12}$ miles

20

0	9
1	7 8 9
2	7 8 9
3	2 2 6 6 7 8
4	0 1 2 2 3 4 7
5	1 2 4 6 8
6	2

1|7 means 17 years
stem = 10 years

21 Perimeter = 28.3 cm

22 a) 76.8
b) 7.68
c) 0.0768

23 a) $5n + 2 = 12$
$5n = 12-2$
$5n = 10$
$n = 2$

b) $4a + 3 = 2a + 8$
$2a = 5$
$a = 2.5$

c) $x = 10$
d) $x = -2.5$
e) i) p^{10}
ii) p^4
iii) p^8

24 £448

25 19.3 minutes

26 $x^2 = 6.2^2 + 4.9^2$
$x^2 = 38.44 + 24.01$
$x^2 = 62.45$
$x = \sqrt{62.75}$
$x = 7.9$ cm (to 1 d.p.)